Contained Entropy :

From Brightness to Darkness

1998-2021

By: Paron Dan Jask IV

Books of Contained Entropy

Book One :
From Brightness To Darkness

I) Light Ramblings - Lighthearted looks at life and love

II) Dark Beginnings - In times of doubt while searching for hope

Book Two :
Uniting Against

III) Dismal Chanting - Slightly darker influenced and seemingly lost
IV) Rebellious Blessings - Literary activism and spiritual questions

Book Three :
A Peace Beyond

V) Meditative Trance - Catharsis and metaphysical exploration

VI) Psychedelic Introspection – Tinges of trippier times from the past
VII) The Lost Works - Once lost and later found poems

VIII) These Songs I Always Sang - Lyrics from music with friends

Copyright 2021
"Anyone who breaks this trust will perish by my pen" – PDJ IV

I) Light Ramblings

1) Für Alix 2/1998
2) Triangular Heart 5/15/2001
3) Love and Live On 5/25/2001
4) Tides of Stride 11/22/2001
5) Gentle Breeze 12/25/2001
6) No Words 6/16/2003
7) The Wild Kingdom Speaks 9/17/2003
8) Ode to Big Red 7/24/2004
9) Bright Light 11/16/2004
10) Wild Monarch 11/26/2004
11) The Slapstick 11/30/2004
12) Hermit Crab 3/26/2005
13) Lightning Storm 6/2005
14) The Fallen Troops 6/23/2005
15) Past the Days 7/31/2005
16) Muse 8/6/2005
17) With Child 8/31/2005
18) Stray 6/21/2006
19) Beautiful Dreams 7/19/2006
20) Requiem for a Meatwad 8/25/2006
21) The Nexus of Her 9/2006
22) Fur Mi Paterfamilias 9/26/2006
23) Illusion 11/3/2006
24) All of the Above 11/14/2006
25) Am I that someone who... 11/14/2006
26) Tractor Beam 11/15/2006
27) -Gravity 1/2/2007
28) Duality 3/8/2007
29) Dye Oceanic 3/8/2007
30) Shine 6/7/2007
31) Vertical 6/8/2007
32) Perma-grin 10/8/2007
33) Second First Day of School 1/2008
34) Painted Glass 10/2008
35) ET Encounters 10/2008
36) Wick 11/10/2008
37) AE 12/24/2008
38) VE 12/24/2008
39) Free Time 12/24/2008
40) Deeply Embraced 9/21/2009
41) Imagining Luck 11/2009
42) Squirtle-San 2/3/2010

43) Para Mi Amigo 8/2010
44) Phoenix 3/6/2011
45) Home Sweet Earth 3/15/2011
46) Grass Break Laying on the Grounds 4/23/2011
47) Insect Buggin' 4/23/2011
48) Virgin Island Sound 4/23/2011
49) Promissio vobis 6/7/2011
50) The Graduate 5/2011
51) Ode to Haney-San's Birthday Guitar 4/19/2011
52) Wisdom roots 7/21/2012
53) Dark Kisses of Chocolate Lavender 7/21/2012
54) Gamma Ray Bursts 2/17/2013
55) Confidences 2013
56) For my sis 4/2013
57) Stone Mountain 9/6/2013
58) A Sonnet for V 3/8/2014
59) Free Songs in the Trees 4/2014
60) Windz 4/11/2014
61) Candle of Camaraderie 9/24/2015
62) Breeze Sonnet 10/5/2015
63) Burning Green 10/2015
64) New Places 11/18/2015
65) Multiple Dimensions 3/7/2016
66) In Honor of Dilly Cat 3/17/2016
67) Truth 5/7/2016
68) Kitty Wanton 6/3/2016
69) Linville Campfire 10/17/2016
70) Strong Roots 10/22/2016
71) Shining on Everything 11/14/2016
72) From under the Bodhi Tree 1/9/2018
73) Taxi to Cali 1/27/2018
74) Gemstones 6/15/2018
75) Finally freed 6/23/2018
76) A Breath of Recursive Reflexes 2/2019
77) Two Sonnets and Six Lines for M.C. 2/25/2019
78) Light Sugar Heavy Cream 6/7/2019
79) Please keep these pages dry 9/26/2019
80) Silas Nicasio 12/2019

81) A Cleaner Table 2/2/2021

82) Echoes Loud 4/14/2021

1) "Für A." early 1998

A night alone we don't talk on the phone

I lay in my bed and weep

A day goes by and I don't look into your eyes

I have trouble falling asleep

If time or chance is all I hold onto

Then this moment I will keep

To think of you every beat of the day

My thoughts flow of the deep

If time or chance may break us apart

I will always hate this cuss

And if I ever see another single pair again

They will always remind me of us

2) "Triangular Heart" 5/15/2001

Your eyes are a two way mirror to the soul

If your love is endless my heart's yours to fold

I could tell from the start that yours is beautiful

We should melt together bodies joined soul to soul

There is no word for as perfect as you are

To write just a stanza would fill up my car

Words just as large as those on this paper

Your love is a drug off which I'd have to taper

Kind of like the pills that I'm coming off of now

Leaving me breathless a heart wrenched holy cow

Rock a bye baby swinging and all

This bow won't break I'll never let you fall

I love you and need you both, cradle and all

3) "Love and Live On" 5/25/2001

Fantastical dreamer whose wishes come true

Here in this moment my heart cries for you

Your blood flows throughout me

pulsations race

Thoughts flow a life

lived with such grace

Dignity infinite of your being so you

Live on in my heart though I don't know you

Sensory through your soul I've seen the sun

Along with the rest of us

in this world we are one

Painless and shameless you left us in ease

Knowing your heart I'll acquaint with you please

Dear Great Grandfather help me to see your love on

Doves may obscure some with

Care and Carry on

4) "Tides of Stride" 11/22/2001

We arise from these tides

This ocean fall called life

On occasion we stride

Upon the dunes to gain height

Though cave-ins may save us from possible defeat

Straying from these waves I fear I shall not meet

A brick road carved out by a life full of nicks

Each taking apart of me burns down my wick
But I know from my scars the paths I shall build

Few particles part with me by others they're willed

So these parts of me I don't miss and not alone I share

At ease I am now but at the time was unaware

Of how difficult the struggle for this can now be

For some structure of form between the sands and the sea

This ocean is ours this sky reflects us to see

Some of those we miss on this day of grateful intrigue

Living angels on winds above heights untold

All of us seeking our great Hera for gold

I've found recently in my life I don't have to look very far

Because most of those we love beat a little to the left

Right within where we are

5) "Gentle Breeze" 12/25/2001

I looked upon floating, ocean's debris

It took a tornado to toss up the breeze

At times we've jumped and others we flee

A rhyme of flow eases mind for all my time freed

Cold gusts biting me drove me so numb

Floating through woods dreamed by me not too dumb

Connected to my quest losing it may key some

Although it looks plastic a metal key is to my drum

I will sail with it flights to villages unknown

Blue sky show me beauty where once it was grown

Blown among this haven wherever snow's strewn

Never a drone in every moment, I'm not alone

Fear not what you don't understand, but seek it

My life lasts forever in my perception, so I'll keep fit

I look up sight to eye with the sky, walking these
Paths we've cleared as I've walked past the trees

You're presence my loved one's I'll always believe

No matter how much sense seems to be within me

We're free,

Merry Christmas to all and to all a gentle breeze.

6) "No Words" 6/16/2003

How can I explain something when there are no words

That could describe the vastness of how little I'm able to tell you

That you haven't already ever heard
I don't just see into your eyes and fall into a trance of love

I sense something surreal far from the harsh reality of

This universal plain that you came from above

This extrasensory experience when you touch me inside

Pieces of our aura dance along with the fluidic rambling of chaos

Inside an open bottle in the space between our eyes
Spine tingles as fortune smiles its wide cheeky grin

Because I wound up in this moment of perception in the same room

That lets the radiance of your sunshine come on in
When will we leave this world to heal on its own for ages

May I follow you to an existence where a gentle wind will lift us

When the author of time seals the fabric and writes our final pages

As I stare to the ceiling I

Only write for and to you trying to reach

To find you and help us ask why

Or why not on a larger scale of how

I feel and the way my heart and mind interact

With yours and how I wish it was now

Looking for any sign of where this eve
May take us to in a hot air balloon

Sailing sun-scaping us to a paradise dream reprieve

Horizons and verizon stretching every single

Directional disorderly interplanetary

Within-most delving of the way they mingle

With themselves and all others within the multiverse

Your heart will always be with me but

If I could one day never see you again there may be nothing worse

7) "The Wild Kingdom Speaks" 9/17/2003

…Words cannot describe how much I love you

Verbs can never hide my feelings for what you do

If I could see through the eyes that shine always to me

I would look into those and reflect on what I could see…

Kittens cats and dogs running through my head

Chickens bats and frogs just as I have said

Are the animals I compare myself to everyday

But the monkeys are the ones who really like to play

Ohhh ohhh ahh ahh eee eee oh

I guess I'm the monkey I said to the toad

But he's just as tired as I always seem to be

But that won't stop me from climbing up this tree…

The monkey is on the ground

The skunk he is walking around

The toad is hopping to and fro

The road is soaring under batty toes

The chicken coocks and cries
The lickin' of the frog's lily pad flies

The kitty is in a tree

She jumps down and sees

Her doggy friend named Ruff

He helps her laugh at different stuff

"Aarf Aarf", said the dog; "Monkey, you are truly amazingly funny."

"Eeek Eeek ", said the monkey; "Bunny is funnier, he plays rain or sunny".

"Ribbit Ribbit", said the frog; "Bunny is great, I'm hoping he'll hop soon our way." "

Rabbit Rabbit", said the parrot; "His name is Rabbit and here he hops dare I say."

"Thh thh", said the bunny; "Hello friends; Kitty are you having lots of fun?"
"Meow Meow", said the kitty; "Yes and I'm glad you came to say hello to everyone."
"Ruff Ruff", said the dog; "Just in jest, I don't mean to say my own name."
"Hee hee hee", said the skunk; "That's okay we still like you all the same."

"Meew Meew", said the kitty; "Hey everyone, let's play a little game."

"Woof Woof," said the doggy; "If we go to get the ball it surely couldn't be lame."

So all the animals in the forest dropped all that they normally do

To amass as a crowd to watch what the teams were starting to get into

The game was played the Furs went first and played until they tired

And in the same warm and thick hollow the animals played until they retired

The End.

8) "Ode to Big Red" 7/24/04

Red haired pixie dancing upon grave

Stone demonstration attention craved

Horns of old cadaverous tear silken skin

Curves of fantastical entrancement I became lost in

Three chord spikes of black leather tones

Breathing her into sunken earthly stones

Coming for me intensely slashing me awake

Into the dream once alive what else will you take

The breath imbibed is empty in substance
Craving consumption of my frontal cortex

You can only digest me under one condition

If you promise me your love of fried chicken

Over that of my raw living flesh

A wing or two of Col. Sanders Best

9) "Bright Light" 11/16/2004

Let us thank all the ones who came from before

They have blessed us and left us with wisdom and lore

The youngest ones grow strong and smart past their days

They're the stars that have landed and shine through the haze

May we clear up the darkness and filter the airs

Cleansing silt through the waters running down mountain stairs

Into the footsteps of fresh trails in frozen dense snow
Patching the connections new friendships we'll grow

Forgive our faithful for living the American dream

And give back to the ones who let us be free

Those who've brought order may have resolved

Perpetual motions in the dirt piles as they've brawled

For a vantage point of hope that hatred will dissolve

Now we face oppositions mounting and tall

Maybe those who've led lately have gone far astray

Let us be weary as we've all made mistakes

This land was claimed for those who come from us

The next day's continuance of departure with trust

Let us thank all the ones who came from before

They have blessed us and given us wisdom and lore

Let us never grow weary of their wishes and our chores

Mobiles dangling from trees that will never become torn

May the lord deliver us as he is able and bless us from above this food and this table

10) "Wild Monarch" 11/26/2004

I melt for you like cheese on toast

You're the kind of girl of which I'd boast

That you find me the guy with the most

Just look into my eyes they are star crossed with hope

Emitting warmth she commits to succeed

In being everything that I could ever need

Four hours a day more than that in the nights

Her image ingrained on eyelids when I cut off the lights

Vessels in the seldom that I stop to stare

At myself in the mirror baggy eyes shaggy hair

I cherish her as I tell myself that she makes me feel so loved

Asking my attention for two feet to be rubbed

No dirty hands my flirty chance is not some windy gust

Only my affection not some short breathing lust

Angelic I can see them in the crisp country skies

That is she is a monarch the most beautiful of butterflies

Drafts her wings flap throughout thinner than the air

Leaving a sweet perfume an aroma that she cares

For me poor me her departure comes so soon

The breeze blowing closing doors she's again left my room

Wild child I wish we could never depart

Wild child I wish to heal your wounded broken heart

While watching the storms and before we may learn

How our sun always warms as our world slowly turns

All I can do is stay true and show her love

She seems so faithful of the world floating above

If she could stay with me I would treat her so right

With nothing to fear as we turn off the light

Somehow I am scared for you but I shouldn't be though

I wish us to show each other how we can grow

I hope it's not but I always question my means

The love from another always seems but a dream

My feet finding failure how may I move onto

To be the one she may stumble upon to

11) "The Slapstick" 11/30/2004

Taste in me I'm a flavor which will shake your scream

I'm the freezer-man who rings the bell up and down your street

A greedy smile as everything I know I've had to pimp
Come to my crowd I pass my symbols to those I meet

When you speak it doesn't matter what you say

An end to this will come to me some darker day

Until then I'll be a shadow stalking in your shade

Cause I'm an animal and baby you're my latest pray

I just want you for emptying my bags

Don't even care if I made you feel so sad

Hope in me that one day I will pray

I'm the man that you'd always hoped could change

It's a slap happy world and I'm the slapstick for whom you'll fall

I just grab a girl anywhere I want I could grab them all
I'll make them pay for how inferior I feel made of clay
No matter what you say I'm not listening or looking at your face
When you speak I compete for volume
Bedroom doors I try to revolve them

Getting off the bus has never been a problem

Puddle of puzzles walk over you try to solve them

12) "Hermit Crab" 3/26/2005

Expel in excess

Immersed in what you express

Emerge from waters

Distance scattered ink blotters

Difference on ledger

Convert the scales of measure

Tip the tender

Break the big spender

Do not answer

Lies ensure the creature

Spattered crimson

Shining remotely in the sun

Dotting and gathering

Collecting in forms wavering

Heated and shelled

Blanketing within itself

Rigid yet brittle

With lines dropping and subtle

Withering alone

Into some new humble home

Shaped from nothing

Resembles stumbling

Falling and stopping
Hiding and watching

Claws flexing

Towards faces perplexing

Take me from this cycle

Ebb and turn of life flow

To sit on your dresser top

In a cage until I dry up

Wish me away

A keepsake dwelling

13) "Lightning Storm" 6/2005

Flying from every direction

Ions of positive polar action

Leaves dance in air current

Flash bulbs from the servant

Splitting crust and forming glass

Everyone out of the pool and fast

Swirling heated and cooling gas

Seeking release from a cast

Predictability on the wrong path

While waiting for the storm to pass

Faking one's heart out of beating past

A close one rumbles the carpet below toes

Explosion breaks numbness and tension grows

Wishing there was someone here to hold

Wondering why she doesn't love me as I was told

14) "The Fallen Troops" 6/23/2005

Everything that you could do
Was to keep your comrades alongside you
Broken from the non-healing wound
At any instant one may turn and find soon
You gave your all to those back home
Memory filling us with undertones
Of Arlington where's room to rest bones
As the shuffling of the fallen chiseled stone
Entrances the young with forms of solitude alone

15) "Past the Days" 7/31/2005

My heart will always remain open to you
From the start I've always loved what you do
I wish we could extend our life spans to great lengths
For more time together a grateful thanks
To whatever gravitates us to each other
The sun the sky our loving Earth Mother
But mainly what beats beneath the chest
I pray for strength and our hearts unstressed
At the end of our days time is all we carry
Long past the days remembering we once married
I will one day close my eyes and when I do
I hope in painless peace I'll be dreaming of you

16) "Muse" 8/6/2005

As my muse you'll never lose

My affection is infinite for you

All I ask is for you to cast

Doubts based upon the past aside

Just hold my arm don't be alarmed

I'll never let them harm you

Let us walk or ride side by side

Through the garden of syncopated tides

By a lake in spring's towing wake

A walk we'll take across to the other side

Please trust in me and in yourself

In the yin and yang of life itself

Just seek happiness in anything

You're a continuous inspiration in all you bring

For me to serenade upon ears deaf

Would be a total waste of my breath

Your hearing so sensitive

My volume reduction will be long lived

I don't want you to hurt but if you do

Remind me on my eyelids with a tattoo

Of darker days forever seen

Echoes of living in a fantasy

That you even want to spend time with me

Is in itself a blessing tender and sweet

Now every girl I measure when I meet

Stands barely up to the top of your feet

I realize my eyes are jaded

Unrealistic expectations faded
When I recognize I'm paralyzed
At least I won't be despised
I carry on undaunted too
As I wish that I was wanted by you

17) "With Child" 8/31/2005

Needlessly awaiting the hours
Elapsed grow towering flowers
Throw shadows into the dim
As the following limb begins
To snake its way up the gate
At an ever increasing rate
Into its final resting place
Looking strongly into my face
Pollination is but a smile
A restless unborn child
Waking its hostess softly
From future filled dreaming
Wide eyed and beaming
Becoming and seeming

18) "Stray" 6/21/06

If I were dead you'd have no scapegoat
If it were all gone no new episodes
Try to place blame for all these sores
An empty attempt to cleanse open pores

If I were dead no one would praise you

You'd have no clue what the crazed can do

Capable of anything as an idiot savant

Except at finding what it is that you want

In your salvation arms closed

Another situation overexposed

So long for now I'll be dead and gone

Until I'm moving towards the paragon

Indifferent to all inherent flaws

Rebelling against all natural law

Overcome selection's heartless view

As I'll never swim near the gene pool

Or see the light come through the skies

Unless her attraction synthesized

Is altered by all points in space and time

A straightened line once combined

With the projections from my eyes

You give me the urge to survive

And the will to stray continuously high

19) "Beautiful Dreams" 7/19/2006

Beauty is truth and sincerity,

beauty is a veneer added to an old table,

a shiny surface covering a past marred with water marks,

a sauntering sprite who approaches you on the eve of midnight, the puppy who looks at you from the window of the pet shop begging for adoption,

the realization that anything is possible by probable odds,
beauty is the realism associated with the power of our imaginations,
beauty is what reflects when you look in the mirror...

and smile because you're truly happy.

20) "Requiem For a Meatwad" 8/25/2006

He always sat in laps

He loved taking naps

He'd run across the room

He'd sniff at your shoes

He'd inhale huge shotguns

Meatwad loved everyone...

I cried when he was gone

We'll miss you Meatwad

21) "The Nexus of Her" 9/2006

So practiced in her faith

and beautiful

I cannot wait

So balanced

a pedestal I will raise

and write a song

Singing her praise

So wrap my thoughts in warmth

Pulled from the cold

And please, never taken away

22) "Fur Mi Paterfamilias" 9/26/2006

Loving,

Keeping a watchful eye,

Focusing all thought upon

The meaning of everything

That it takes to keep a child from harm,

Strong hands to reach out

To tiny ones clenching at fingertips,

Safety in the pack

Of sentient guards

Never alone,

Looking over at

Patterns forming freely,

Never alone

As anywhere may become home

A tome among

a volume well known.

23) "Illusion" 11/3/2006

An apparition

Offset by it's vision

Casting reflective at angles aside

So obtuse

Obnoxiously aloof

Drastically by my remorse I abide

Only illusion can heal this confusion

Tricking myself understanding how it felt

When she walks my way through the dark
Placing a hand on my forehead and then

Reaching lips for mine her soft fingertips

Slip me from a cage that held me enraged

A selfless prophecy of illness

In secrecy I will fulfill this

Mind bending

Mending

In a past life

My path was once rife

Mindful steps of comfort forward

Only now reversed

As everything grows worse

Shrinking from what I walk towards

24) "All of the Above" 11/14/2006

Lit up by thoughts of you
The window's growing thin
I've had a lot to do
Now I'm wondering where you've been

Hope you've seen days of happiness
Even though we've been apart
Hope you know you've been missed
Just like pieces of my heart

Always carried with you
So many things remind me
A storm, a butterfly, a tissue
And all the best of times we've seen
I'll always have a place for you
I'll never ever forget you
If you ever need someone to love
Because of all of the above
Claim me before I'm taken
Let us reawaken
Looking into each other's eyes
At every sun's set and rise

25) "Am I that someone who…" 11/14/2006

Am I that someone who…

Could never lie to you

Would never want you to do something you didn't want to do

Respects the way you feel

Always listens when you have something to say

Genuinely cares about you

Enjoys spending time with you

Can make you blush

Could protect you from being hurt

Can dry your tears

Listens when you've said no

Supports you

And loves you with all of his heart?

Whose life you could ultimately bring

a sense of direction, meaning, and balance to?

26) "Tractor Beam" 11/15/2006

Beth, you took away my breath

How could I ever forget?

When you looked at me with a smile

From a distance you caught my eye

Set me to silence with a touch

In response you drew me much

Away from a sense of distraction

To find a purposeful action

To forget of you would be a sin

But the question lingers,

Will I ever see you again?

27) "-Gravity" 1/2/2007

Up is down I brought the sky to the ground

In upper atmospheres I float around

Being on the floor I knew there was more

So I walk on ceilings

Jumping below the tops of doors

Stealing my way around like a drug

Holding a mirror to watch the ground above

To see where I should be

Living free in negative gravity

28) "Duality" 3/8/2007

A duality that transcends the strength of singularity

Combined forces seeking stable balance

A proton and neutron in a nucleic bond

Against all odds immeasurable

Flowing together through the seas of chaos

Yet bringing forth a form familiar

Unique in its composition

A breath only breakable upon expiration

A half life that lasts twice a lifetime

A moment in history where time slows down

Cycling perceptions in congruence

A duality is one momentous continuation of time that flows like water down tributaries, into lakes and rivers then eventually back into the air to rain upon the heads of those who come next.

Welcome to this world, may your strength hold you together and may your days of love last for an eternity glorious.

A self referential string that cannot be broken and that can only grow stronger with time.
An experience, an experiment of experts
A duality of togetherness, a transition into the pairing of one.
Bringing meaning that stands together and alone but never in solidarity.

29) "Dye Oceanic" 3/8/2007

Merci Mademoiselle

Your love is divine and shimmering

As a jewel lost on the oceans below

The common density of a stone

Found by my dive into the unknown
In a trench I was never shown

Happened upon by me, I alone

Never thought to expand this wondrous discovery

A crossroads of astounding symmetry

Bringing about the changes, from a life led so lonely

Now nothing but a path to happiness leads

And the years by myself that have been following me

Become unattached as she will set my soul free

Now I only need to find out where and when could she be

Coming and turning my sun's reflection blue to green

30) "Shine" 6/7/2007

>
> Finding a pearl
>
> In shells curled
>
> Between the coral
>
> Among sands swirled
>
> By current trends
>
> I will not bend
>
> But if you were my girl
>
> I'd feel like the whole world
>
> Is to stumble upon
>
> A far deeper bond
>
> And a gracious touch would shine miracles

31) "Vertical" 6/8/2007

>
> I'd never hurt you
>
> because I'd be less a man
>
> I'll clean your wounds
>
> until your scars disband
> Disappearing in contrast
>
> just like the last
>
> Following no longer
>
> Bully buried nine feet under
>
>
> I would never take from you
>
> unless you held out open hands
>
> For me to place my heart into
>
> Without making plans

With half for me, half with you

I just want to understand

The only thing I'd take is a chance and a stand

32) "Perma-grin" 10/8/2007

I'm wearing my smile

On the outside for style

I let it shine

The glaring bright lie

Blind and tense

Winding your senses

Around my finger

The deception lingers

'Til the end for some

Inside I am numb

A slight reputation

For sensory deprivation

A lack of affection

Has turned my complexion

From flesh to plastic

A shifting so drastic

I will never again

Take off this perma-grin

Not even for a while

So I'm wearing my smile

And letting it dry

Underneath the inside

33) "Second First Day of School" 1/2008

As new as becoming reacquainted with familiar movement

After years of slumber as an objective subject

In seclusion from the waking of walking through the sun's rays

Being split by the projections of the treetop bay

Awash in lines and lulled, sifting the tides

Breaching the surface with shifting divides

Once on sands many have crossed

Now granules at the feet of the embossed

34) "Painted Glass" 10/2008

In the broken eyes of jesters

Looking through the painted glass

For the things that matter the most

For the suits that suit you best

On bent knees of the trusting

Search for the touch that is blessed with success

With the righteous for the freaks

As the creature I stare at will kill me

So divided so holy

As the creature I stare at becomes me

35) "ET Encounters" 10/2008

>
> I'm your alien baby
>
> Bring me to he who leads
>
> And let me prepare you
>
> The human race cannot be freed
>
> From the torture of dissection and impregnation
>
> With a hybrid seed of our experimentation

36) "Wick" 11/10/2008

>
> You bring a smile to my face and a mischievous fire
>
> Like a candle burning from both ends
>
> That hasn't been lit in ages, suddenly self set ablaze
>
> Your voice is a whisper
>
> A gentle caress of attention and care
>
> Echoing as I remember, through reflections of smoke
>
> All is not barren as I had once believed
>
> Illuminate this thought, throw shadows on my walls
>
> As approaching flames consume all doubt

37) "A.E." 12/24/2008

>
> Always so loving as
>
> Meaningful times find us,
>
> You're
>
> Everyone's
>
> Dearest sweet young

Woman

And one of two sisters who

Rule and are cool too

Don't ever doubt yourself 'cause you're

Smart and everyone really loves you

38) "V.E." 12/24/2008

Very much

A sister who makes me

Laugh

Every time we hang out,

Reminding me of my own sense of humor

I know you'll end up doing

Everything you'd ever wish to

Do. Like a supernova

With the future, so bright for you

As graceful and fluid in motion as you are

Remember, I'll always love you

Don't forget that the blood we all

Share runs deep with wisdom and thicker with time

39) "Free Time" 12/24/2008

You've always been there for us

Always will

I'll share this still framed image

with you of this,

I know more of what it takes

to be the man I will and am

Through your care and time

I'll always cherish our memories
And never take anything for granted

Wishes of the world will find me

Soon I'll meet with synchronizing seas

The time has never been sweeter,

flowing more determined and free

40) "Deeply Embraced" 9/21/2009

Upon meeting, there was more said between our eyes

Than my words can- accurately describe

Hopeful approaches at dusk-time

That in searching I'll never find

But she discovered me

Among things I failed to see

Subtle and personally, a deprivation of affection

Has over the years trapped me in forms of isolation

Wrapped over eyes was a disguise now realized

That kept me company but alone for much time

Now she has uncovered this as my identity

Secretly has become more of me,

In a way that is set free by continuing certainty

That nothing is wrong, I am more complete

Doubting was wrong of me and now obsolete

At least in ways that stifle my senses

Trapping myself behind electrical fences

The voltage was cut when she came near

Now I have no fears if she will stay here

And I will too, if stars align connected to us

Today and years from now I will always trust
Never holding a thing against her or ever judging her

Even if we grow apart and end up with others

Never is it in me to ever mistreat her

Or lie to, ignore her, or take for granted either

The fact that if nothing happens, this is only written word

But if it happens for both of us, I'd love her deeply as one could

41) "Imagining Luck" 11/2009

So high I know why

Your eyes look so beautiful tonight

The ways you look into mine

Reminds me of a simpler time

Where I don't have to try

And all is well and all is love

As the luckiest man to ever be by your side

42) "Squirtle-San" 2/3/2010

The Siamese in your looks

intermingles with your dog-like tendencies

Nudging your nose,

then biting,

to show us you love, you own

Fetching jingling plastic balls

and pseudo dead mice

Your meow more like a rattle

a tremble singing notes of splendor

but your smile more radiant
you drink from my water cups

when I look away, dipping there

and your paws are cold this time of year

You curl up hugging my arm

each night purring of dancing dreams and

it reminds me of all the moments

where i was your pet, you my friend

will always be a warm happy ball of fuzz

Close to my heart and snoozing,

head curled on my open hand

43) "Para Mi Amigo" 8/2010

I couldn't believe this as no one deserved it less,

You handled a massive weight which burst the seams

Everything shifted on all of us and the ground fell out

This crimson cake left before us as a testament will wash away into the past,

cleansed of fortune, good or bad.
Separating us from external forces,

hoping and never worrying.

If you had fallen completely,

an emptiness would have befallen all of our friends

If you could not lift a leg again,

there still would be many paths you'd cross.

However you pass the thresholds beyond comprehension my friend, may it be many decades down lines, undivided and with little pain.

/

However you may find yourself, resilience is the only way

I couldn't tell the injustice of your situation, it's far too unfair
But whatever obstacles you'll face, I know you will overcome them
You have the strength of mind and spirit for it my friend, for I have seen it
Just use your experiences wisely and pass them on to others
When the time is right,

You will probably help more people than you could ever imagine

By just holding on, throughout the most difficult times

Life is sometimes about

Proving to ourselves, we can never be held down

So don't ever let anything do this,

Just push it all away

But don't ever push away those who care most about you

Just know that you've got a lot of friends this way

Who know you, met you just a few times, or just know of you

On their behalf, I can say sincerely

Everyone really wants to see you succeed, in anything you do

And whatever may ail you these days, it will pass as all does

Just as your misfortunes will pass in time

But we'll always be here and faith will mend all afflictions

So don't ever worry, my friend

These words are but a gift for you, as is life

44) "Phoenix" 3/6/2011

Awakening something so primal,

The essence of attraction itself,

Slaps me in the face one moment, in anger,

Then embraces me lovingly in the next,

Like a temptress of death and love.

Hair on fire, eyes of the sky,
Like the backdrop for massive clouds,

Swirling in the distance beyond her.

Reflecting in her eyes, a crystalline entrancement,

One that has seen the sun and come back, immaculately intact

Like a phoenix which never burns out, but blazes on,

Searing in your soul and seeing light from eons back, refracted and stunning.

45) "Home Sweet Earth" 3/15/2011

Visceral images so divine in light

Shedding, falling from

Earthen forms of sight

Casting a shadow on all which I see

Yet in a brilliance of mattering, only to me

'Tis the seer's tale of

Martian woe

Shutting the candle-lit room's door

To an end of a chapter, an ode to a time

Lancing the lash over the veins of my prime

Saturn's moons and an eon of storms
Could not prepare me for the ways of the worlds
Compared not, to the heat of our blood
An artery gushes the hues of crimson flood

A knife of

Jupiter stabbing,

And Neptune's full of kinks...
Pluto is judgmental and Uranus,

Well that just stinks.

Venus is my lover, she bathes me in her dreams
Of greenhouse gases asphyxiating and boiling at the seams
And Mercury is a liar, she dwells beside the sun
Begging for an atmosphere and coming all undone.

/

Me, I am lonesome

And calling out her name

Haven't met her yet in time

But it's all the same

Sticking to my reason

Refilling knowledge is my way

And keeping the asteroids and comets

Quite far off at bay

Still I'm drinking from the dewdrops

Forming on the green morning pines

Kicking up the red clay

And feeling fine all the time

46) "Grass Break Laying on the Grounds" 4/23/2011

The woods in daytime

taking some breaks

In the canopy above

Shining through

To the whims of heady foods
Heads used to the refuge

of wearing the skies

and being among the breezes

The trees and me are sharing the daze

Of smells rich with Earth and dirt

Turned to mud, meeting of boot's pant legs and skirts

As the crowd shakes and spasms, trance-lacing

In tune to the time within and taking it, breaking

Four twenty minutes

Ahead of this year and behind the lines

Beneath the dew's peers

Red clay damp under my feet

Laying on a straw mat among my roots

Dr. Ew and Yoda on grass

Drawing near and past the last

Trudging through stirring up the past

And smoking air, breathing in the lawn

Walking forwards in mucky footings

Sure of it, peace will be found here

On the vines, monkeys swing 'round clear

Grabbing too, I join them grooving on down

One with the rhythm, beating the ground

47) "Insect Buggin'" 4/23/2011

Bugs don't bug me

Ticks and eye-flies love me

Dehydrate taking my beating

Rhythmic pulse cannot ever

Leave a leaf of dew above my tongue

Primal dryness of words new and young

Exhausted and seething

Hearing the lack of fear

I leave behind

Ghost limbs of attaching

Left all the times

Behind mine eyelid

Perceptual chimes

Open to everything

Earthling and kind

48) "Virgin Island Sound" 4/23/2011

Sounds of the Caribbean

Ring to the days,

five years back

And in the thick of it

Homeland in soul again

bringing me forwards

Not as much reversed as before

She commands it

With a chanting look of seriousness

at the indignation of my being

Freezing us, in temptations reeling

As they dance and twirl

In colored hoops and smiling

High in the air's cooling charms

Returning smiles only out of my mojo

I rerun a mile, hiking to our dojo

I lay on the ground, looking up to her

Mother Nature helping me

Playing with words

Listening to the truth stir

Clouding up the festivus

Uniting of life, most grand "intuis"

The moves we dance, leaving us fulfilled

The songs we sing, carry over the hills

All we imbibe, finding us nourished

In spiritual fire, forever flourished

49) "Promissio vobis" 6/7/2011

Seems as if, you are anything but a contradiction personified

Deeming it necessary, as no one can be easily quantified

Qualities counting the brilliance of times

I say tally nothing,

just rally-drifting through high tides

Flow of the beaches

in the summers of our lives

These waters reflect eyes, knowingly kind

Wittiness compliments you, in diligence of minds

They may not know yet, but it's the most curious of times

Winding and whirling, wavering in lines

Wish me away, I'd stop and never fall apart

If you would want to,

Please ask me anything anytime, I start this with art

and if you write me back I promise, never to hurt or scar

Especially your dream's seams,

deep within the folds of Belle's beautiful heart

50) "The Graduate" 5/2011

Stepping across the ledge

Over new thresholds again

Will bring you further, and farther

To where your wishes never end.

Universal and granted

A challenge of hills, slanted

Towards a spring board bounce

That will keep you perpetually free.

Your jumps may be higher

Than the other's hopeful fires

But the flames are far below

Your dancing feet.

You're the kind who coals can't char

My cousin, you'll go far

S'long as you keep the grounds

Close beneath your feats.

Keep on as you have, go for undergrad

Before you know it, you'll be a PHD.

51) "Ode to Haney-san's Birthday Guitar" 4/19/2011

Pluck her softly

She'll stay with you

Maybe even knocked up a bit for awhile

If you thrash her around
She'd get pretty banged up

But as long as you respect her and honor her sound

She will always love you regardless of how,

on her strings you pound

just be easy, slow on down now

Just make sure if she gives you some back-talking reverb,

You tell her to get back in the studio and make you damn some recordings

Chop chop, to the shop of the rock,
Barefoot and beautiful, with tone that won't stop

Bet she likes to be played slowly and like a gentleman

If you ever ask her to bring a friend, she'll hopefully be eager

Willing and able to play anytime she wants to please you

Don't be a player, never so forceful

Let her play you too, an act so trustful

Just make sure you act as a guitar too,

Giving and taking as those lovers would do

Show her more than is required,

and she will be a companion, endlessly admired

Setting her on the stage and burning them with fire

The ears of the listeners with sunburst in arrays

Volumes echo off walls,

Without ever any sudden or lasting decay.

52) "Wisdom roots" 7/21/2012

Passing on the wisdom of times

Grass is greenest on both of the sides

There's never a hill on either grounds of consciousness

Believing our roots are planted so strongly all over the east
A free land's dreams varied individual with righteousness

We still walk paths through a wooden fern grove covered in fleeting peace

Passing forwards forever we bare no force of resistance towards one's freed ease

Deep in the ground some things congenitally absorbed manifesting
We never forget the chances we've taken and the choices made waking

Birds adorn your window whistling morning's day grown and glowing

Monuments set in sunlight's love as much ethereal rays eternally are placing

53) "Dark Kisses of Chocolate Lavender" 7/21/2012

Thank you as all of our televisions are off for a good book or three

And any day now love or murder is at the tip of my fingers finding glee

There's so much more to the pictures of us hanging around anyone can see

Rubbing her shoulders after a long day drudging over while minding fleets

Kisses like cherries rich with tartness and strokes our hands entangled freed
Changeling for the evening leggings rolled on like an elastic coating fantastic
Turning it up and me onto my knees begging and willing to go every and anywhere
For her, she brings it all to a stop as all the background noise once had faded
The flowers whitened, gown of dress enlightened brightening
She slinks off her skirt dropping to the floor of wonderful inviting

Seductively she pulls me towards bedrooms thousands of degree in heat

We make love like wild beasts for hours on most days our paths cross

There is friction between as we fit together and stick to each other

As lovers often do there's dancing at dawn in a love cocoon sweating

She makes all other ladies pale in comparisons not worth one's weighing

Her scent of dark lavender and chocolate with a fire breathing bed layered and laid upon

Satin and lingerie she teases all senses in ways words would never be worthy of

Bringing a silence to my soul as everything else would be truly whole

54) "Gamma Ray Bursts" 2/17/2013

Brilliance in you is like never fading away from

I love being in your lights while I play on my old drums

I light for you the same stage of the stars on the twos and the one

For our supernovas will be red dwarfs, spiraling disks,
Our gamma bursts emissions for light years of millennia
The rising of crests within my heart red too, wishes
My love for you first was lit near Valencia

And air of the mountains we roam are the guides to our souls

My loneliness from me is the best thing you've ever stole

I love when the smiles you show light as I play on my old drums

Times of inspirations hiding from nowhere, togetherness comes

55) "Confidences" 2013

I am confident

In our confidences

You are inspiring

In all music's muses

I am open to all

As in a ways of pathways

You are a sweet mountain lady

As in, I'll love you under darkest days

I am the one who beckons you

In a way. I'd always do

Everything and anything you ask me to

For there is much to learn from you.

If I ask for inspiration, it's however I am found

Always thought I was laying drowned, dead on the ground

56) "For my sis'" 4/2013

First off

I love you

is all I know how to start off

Never said it enough

but either way

I don't love my stuff

But things and stuff

come and go, yet family

Now that's a beautiful thang

In all ways and here and now

These songs I always sang.

/

Such a thing from us

as if was never heard

So many a thing

there always was to learn

These things of which

I know for you are true

The times of love the world

has ahead to offer you

/

For you are the sun

I've written this from the moon

Sitting here on mountain top

Standing with a flag for you

When the Earth's in fray

in so many ways

beyond the blankets

We all hid under in younger days

Hurricanes came our ways

but we found ground for longer stays

the ground here cannot betray

Our footings firm we always knew the way

These trodden grounds have lit up my face

realize we are awakening time and space

We can turn the night away from its dismay

And the haze lifts, sifting a unbalance portrayed

the sun always rises and sets every day

While we rotate around it our own unique ways

57) "Stone Mountain" 9/6/2013

Mountains are moved by love

Formed from the dust blown in

We all drift towards each other

As lifelong friendships like family

Cherish the love you have

You both a perfect pair

May your days glow light

And your nights burn aware

As I drink to you both at this gathering here

We are reminded that none of us are alone

We all come together to celebrate an end to tears

Our combined energies will eliminate all fear

I couldn't be happier to go to the Mountain of Stone

To wish you both the best and a warming of your home

58) "A Sonnet for V" 3/8/2014

I love a fierce and fiery woman
Full of passionate seeking
With eyes open wide to the world
Without ever accepting defeat
She shares my disdain
For atrocity, for innocents falling
For what else may perish
Without a hint of hope being lost?
I love a fierce and fire breathing woman
Filling my dreams, seeking
Intense as suns pulling in planets
Our gravitation has recently crossed
Now I want to share everything
Knowing nothing could ever be lost

59) "Free Songs in the Trees" 4/2014

"Chansons gratuites
dans les arbres"

Curves like a sea
Swerves mystery
When she swings along trees
Holding vines just like me
In my trees while playing flute

I had found some fruit
Sweet as the melon moon

And glistening wax the sun

Beads flow sweaty truth

Now a sub-nature monkey like me

Would never ever bite at thee
But I would lick citric sweat

As we are sucking away at all stress

From tips to our tongues

The frost would nip some

But even at absolute degrees

The juice would not let us freeze

Combined in our smoothies
The reaction between you and me
And the pulps when we're free
To hangout in each other's trees
Yours grow the fruit most sweet
And with little means as we have meat
Our gardens grown complete
Every season sings songs free to dream

"Chaque saison

chante des

chansons libres

de rêver"

60) "Windz" 4/11/2014

Time to grind and leave no traces of my losses behind

Time to rhyme, retrieve and rewind, then fast forward into all time

But it all mellows out as there can be no doubt

Only do and done

and never could be dumb

Fell into crumbs

as I floundered behind the drums

Then found my way back

centre again

Is there some knack relaxed

For knowing

We should have more freedoms intact?

When who are the next targets?

For mistakenly we are borrowed

And churned under into chum gleefully

Only words can destroy it as emergencies have been forbid

Wax and wane in any direction the windz, we sail, dissolve into brill grim

When life has no value you control, how can you empower us not to overpower you all?

Words are no weapon only used with Satyagraha

To convert all enemies into friends

Only with words can we make our final refrains

Now we have the camera angle's lens

One day no one will have to hurt again
With words which truly bring life to and anew

Now as I cry and the wind's outside

Still move through walls and dry my sight

Nowhere have I seen so beautiful

But in Cary's ground, here is my home town

And we should all work to keep her brand-old

Our connections here go back thousands of years

To the ones who knew Nature's boundless love

Now we must carry on what we know and write

We must keep burning for them their brightest of lights

Because the freest of all, were always in every way so right

61) "Candle of camaraderie" 9/24/2015

I'll try to stay fresh and so fly towards the cool Autumn breezes of the night's skies

I've asked every question and I still don't why so a singular direction towards my bed tonight

I'll wind myself down the best I can try and find myself drowned in sleepiness eyes

With time I will surmise my dreams tonight may become a reality in all parts of my life

If I never had a waking of peace in light then the karma behind would never burn so bright

The wick never ends ceasing delight because I know through my friends no love is denied

62) "Breeze Sonnet" 10/5/2015

Haven't known her all that long although I am sure

I've met no one as wonderful my intentions clearly pure

Eyes shining like blue sapphires shimmering in the sun

Sparkling radiance so beautiful her spirit has become

From my chest I feel a flow fluttering and warm

The best I can do is help her shelter from the storms

There must be some lull in time a calming peace within

The balances we seek in life our hearts may begin

To find ourselves intertwined may seem too bittersweet

We met in weirder circumstances instead of passionate heat

They say I'm sweet yet mischievous as is all my past

I throw this paper's wings to the winds flying like the last

With no expectations for the hope my loneliness will pass

63) "Burning Green" 10/2015

Sun goes up sun goes down

Swings to the other side of town

Stars glow bright moon hangs proud

To light up the lines of the city's gown

She shines bright the skyline shroud

Spillin' out to the streets in music loud

Darkens the pearl upon her necklace shines

We love outside of where the image lies

Sparking light behind our eyes

I love her more in morning delight

Have not a name for it

No words can say for me

I love you like destiny

Burns bright with fire green

Her sparkle seems it never fade in the night

To focus a flash in moments of insight

She has a tractor beam that pulls me inside
Never hesitating to blow my mind

Having not some name for it

No words express what I have felt

I love you like destiny

Burning bonfire green

64) "New Places" 11/18/2015

The world is new to you

Open your eyes surprise it's true

You've got a good family who love you

Who'll always support all you do

One day we will laugh

One day we will walk

I smile when I wonder

What you'll say when you talk

You'll ask a thousand questions

Answers are to seek

You could climb any mountain

To its highest peaks

Mommy and Daddy will show you love

Wipe every tear from your cheeks

And every night you can dream

Of new places you can reach

65) "Multiple Dimensions" 3/7/2016

You are beautiful

in a multitude of ways

In your smile

Telling truths you say

Your deep beliefs

And strength of faith

I see unique beauty

in your soul, your grace

Your eyes ablaze

with fire of passion free

You have lived

Experiences I have never seen

I know a deep respect

I love who you've become

As times have passed

My heart beats for you on my drums

Your company

kind, warm and inviting

Knowing you

has always been inspiring

You are beautiful

in a multitude of ways

And I notice more

of them every glowing new day

66) "In Honor of Dilly Cat" 3/17/2016

Orange with stripes

ate the faces off his prey

Dilly Cat used to

keep Squirtle company everyday

They were homies

of the posse SSP

Kitties ran the streets

of Sorrell back in history

Dilly was the chillest

one never to be forgotten

He was a sweet old

barn cat loved and spoiled rotten

I miss him so much already

he is now at peace

No longer in pain

his spirit has been eased

I hope in kitty heaven he is free

to be the king of the yard released

67) "Truth" 5/7/2016

You're so humble, but this needs to be said though

You're the kindest, most understanding person I know

You have an endless amount of love to give

Grace, strength and honesty in how you live

Supporting your family through all we do

You have taught me patience and always truths

Helped me through the darkest of days

Now I just want to thank you with loving praise

You are the most important person in my life

You have kept me on the path of doing right

A promise I can keep because it's true

I will always love you and be there for you

68) "Kitty Wanton" 6/3/2016

The more years you chill here by my side

You are the feline queen of the castle

The leader of your pride

I find more ways to admire

Your youthful stride and love it grows

There is a special place inside my heart

Where you will always reside

I treasure our moments

You seem so zen-like

And then all of the sudden...

You attack

To show your dominance

Your ownership

Of all around you

Since the time

I have shared my rooms with you

You have enlightened me so

I love your ferocity

As much as your fuzzy sweet side

You have a kinship with me

A feline sister who brightens my life
Thank you for needing me

Just as much as I have needed your company

And your spirit is from and among the stars

There is no other kitty who compares to you

Has a glow within which burns with such fusion

69) "Linville Campfire" 10/17/2016

A circular barrier from the cold

A pit ablaze lined with stones

I stare all night into orange glow

Lit a small yellow light it grows

Feeding the flames chunks of wood

Sizzles and pops smoking up good

If there was ever anything I understood

I contemplated by the fire all which I could

Living outside like children of the Earth

A tent and all provisions aside a hearth

I never found any hope inside of a church

Although here by the waterfall and gorge

Out here in the open I find freedom's rebirth

Love hiking my way every towering viewpoint

Higher than me and the clean cool air anoints

My lungs fill with spirits pulling on joints

This Fall greenery and scenery appoints

Me as a guide of hollow's thicket within

The mountain maps warped, my compass grins

We walk across pages writing with feet like pens

This all leaves me longing to return here again
Soon logs we're burning are coals dead and dim

Let's pour water and stir then retire to the tent

Sleep in the chill as all heat has burned out spent

We drive home in the morning with campfire scent

The flames have receded to whence they were kept

70) "Strong Roots" 10/22/2016

This tree has strong roots

There is clear path ahead of you

I'm sure you'll be

An awesome little dude

An old pair of good genes

Comforting and loving scenes

With the most amazing

And wonderful parents to be

May you hold a creative fire

Read beyond your years inspired

Work hard to be prolific

And intellectually aspire

Let's all hike the world

Help lead them to peace

The best thing for us

We are born to be free

I really hope to be

Like my uncles before me
They are kind and speak brilliantly

Now I must live more carefully

I love you all,

Let's live like our dreams

71) "Shining on Everything" 11/14/2016

You have always inspired me

Brilliant, scientific, forever curious

An intellect so refined and natural

Always seeking new findings in every field

You helped me discover

The importance of seeking education

To arise from humble and difficult beginnings

I aspire to make you proud in my ways and studies

You and Grandma

Always taught me spiritual wisdom

Our church is the only one I feel at home in

I always found so much peace alongside you both there

I will never forget

How you have always been there for us all

Your stability and strength and the impact you both have

On our family and community is beyond anyone else

May we all live with respect and love

You have always led us, and from within us all

We will always dream, spirits free to call

I find peace knowing you will be eased
In the realization we'll all soon be freed

Grandpa John,

You will always inspire

Your warm heart of the sea

Is the love of our family

A bright hope found shining on everything

Which lights all of our lives and helps us to see

72) "From under the Bodhi Tree" 1/9/2018

I've never felt more alone
Then when I had no place of home
In all I roamed and palindromes
Kept a painful soreness in my bones

Until I've found this whole new start
I feel unleashed from within my heart
My family I love to reconnect the dots
Within my soul all aching stops

Of how things are and should be
A new balance and hope released
Fear has faded replaced with knowing
Of who I am and where I'm going

One whose closeness always inspires
Her love a power which is higher
A natural rhythm to our lives flows
I see clarity because she knows
Without her influence I would be so lost
My emotions and self-truths aside to be tossed
Always will be there for her as she is for me
She first held my tiny hand under the Bodhi Tree

73) "Taxi to Cali" 1/27/2018

I don't care the cost
Nothing can be lost
Clouds brush the sea
On a taxi to Cali
Never felt so prepared
To breathe a different kind of air
Like a blanket of deepest joy
Freedom breezes to enjoy
Spirit and mind at ease
Feels like we are spreading peace
Planted roots within my grounds
Can go walking we have found
Within new places I will bury
My feet from red clay sanctuaries
Into a new transplanted state
Inspired passing through this gate
Ocean's winds of concentrate
She caresses my hand lights my face
A candle's birth a hearth's been placed
A flame afloat a glowing stage
Looking to the East from the West
Would melt the wax of dripping content
This brightness grows within my soul
The ocean reflects us I long to hold
Her close enlightenment seems I'd see
Now I must save up for a taxi to Cali

74) "Gemstones" 6/15/2018

Strict with a newfound patience for life

Once seeking luxuries then humbled of pride

She helped teach me to learn and morals I abide

Becoming an example of how to take things in stride

She has helped me in ways I cannot thank enough

Scraping me off the ground in latest patches of rough

Supposedly I just needed to be more tough

Going easier on myself I didn't really have to jump

She gave back more than was ever given to her

Empowering and inspiring those around her for sure

Grandma helped me to see life's worth living for

And with that which I value, I will never be poor

Pain and suffering immobilized does not carry on

Now that she's reunited with Grandpa John

If that's at all possible on this ball we balance upon

Flung through the cosmos chanting our spirit songs

I sometimes wonder when I'll be going gone
Then I reassure myself the waiting won't be long

Tears drip on this page though not of despair

But of love and knowing she will always be there

As long as my soul stays intact and aware

Impermanence leaves the physical as dust in the air

But memories crystallize that everyone shares

And these are the most valuable gems we could ever wear

75) "Finally freed" 6/23/2018

No longer in pain, nothing's the same

From crazy to sane, balance attained

A pattern's layers, laid over the plain

Flying the skies, derived from the change

About and around, one end to another

Connecting the dots while dreaming a lover

I must now seek to help my own brothers

Feeling as if I lived as a drunkard

Discounting spiritually what you had said
Has left me broken as a gypsy misled

By myself I am lost without my own bed

Sleeping daydreaming and eerie with dread

Wish I could have reached out to you more

Often times shredded, my spirit so torn

A hopeless despair overwhelms with allure

Shattering ideals and shadowing the shores

These sands we have crossed leave trails of our peace

Shimmering blue and enlightening the beach

Transcending the tides, how far can we reach?

Further and farther than we could ever see

Beyond these horizons and over the trees

I know you're looking over me, finally freed

76) "A Breath of Recursive Reflexes" 2/2019

If I break off a part of my self for you
To share the strengths I have nothing to prove
Have walked such paths before and I always lose
When I go it alone there is nothing to choose

Such traps I've set ensnare my feet every time

And lost in darkness hollow my spirit in a bind
In contemplation these winds of ashes scatter mine
I entered knowing the decimation I would find

This urn of future days dismayed from my play

An actor smiling on the surface of disarray

The stage was set divisively split and portrayed

As if nothing mattered regardless of what I say

Can I muster up the courage fearlessly for you?

I'm too worried about having nothing to do

An idle state with my mind set in lieu
Of all which I stand for humming the blues

Screaming to the heavens harnessing the heat

A core of magnetism gripping my feet

Not much room left to write on this sheet

The ways of karma counteracting defeat

I hope and wish for you to find your peace

Love has always brought us new release

From a cage of captivity and utter defeat
Breaking from a mold stronger than concrete
/
You have a wealth of love within your heart

And everyone around you has broken apart
In the past, we must keep on finding new starts
However you may heal you must shut out the dark

A dismal abyss I've learned not to identify with

Sucks out our souls as if through our lips
Seething and grinding my teeth down to bits
She kissed me demonically in ignorant bliss

I have hope this incantation will keep them at bay

An invocation of protection, a prayer sent your way

Everything I have ever known from birth 'til today

Frees me from the shackles of impending decay

Now finding great hope you will always overcome

So you will not wallow in desolation feeling numbed

Learning from my mistakes and pitfalls of being dumb

Experience at times has caught up with me and won

This is no contest a ladder of life

A hierarchy of peoples is illusory strife

Such dissolves with perception of time

A new perspective of heart beats and rhyme

We must protect you from every ill

Negative person which lingers 'round still

Keeping the peeping toms from your windows

Will be the task of my fire of fusion and cinders

/

Confusion abandon and greater loss

Will be tossed aside with clarity embossed
On braille or in dreams we have much to read

To learn how to cinch up and restitch our seams

You won't ever have to again hurt yourself
Because the young lady emerging has found new health

Our shells are a Hell which must be broken free

Would do anything for you as I bare my whole life for all to see

Naked and shivering in the cold February breeze

Rained on and soaked I'm soon to freeze

When I return to my roots in the bottom of the sea

I'll make sure to carry an extra tank along with me

So you don't lose your breath expressing relief
And love finds you never restless and always serene

77) "Two Sonnets and Six Lines for M.C." 2/25/2019

I) "Soul Purpose as the Clouds Part"

My soul's sole purpose is to heal all your wounds

I live for those around me even for you too

As long as we've known, our paths barely crossed

Though your presence at once left my spirit embossed

With an impression so honest and true from the start

Only in sincerity the expressions of my heart

Your aura so bright it blends with the stars

I've been lost in the darkness behind Mars

Been quite the space cadet for many years drifting run strong

But my feet walking on red clay is where they belong

When I slow myself down the hourglasses pause

As I remember your smiles and the laughter you caused

A brighter light of warmth which is never obscured

By the clouds or my notions of doubting my own words

II) "Painting on Every Surface"

When I question all odds against me in fear

Then I know nothing of life except endless tears

Blurring all my pages with trembling lines

Chicken scratch writing like a doctor in my mind

I don't need a metronome to breath jazz timings

Not every measure has it's porcelain linings

Exhaling a sigh for the wintertime dull

Loneliness seems a cliché, a tiring droll

If one day you have found me please grasp my hand

Because you truly inspire this boy as a man

I'd paint every surface for you with the flick of a brush

An honest portrayal of a sun you can trust

If reading this helps to calm you with ease

I'd hold you close meditating for peace

III) "A Dream Luminescent"

If bioluminescence would glow through the sea

Then surely it would be lit by your soul's beauty

If never another finds me the rest of my life

It would even be an honor just to dream you my wife

One from which I would never ever want to wake

A slumber of finding new faith in new fates

78) "Light Sugar Heavy Cream" 6/7/2019

Light sugar with heavy cream

Helps me awaken from my dreams

Four cups later starts my daydreaming

Brown and so beautiful of taste

Love my buzz for me so true

And I'll always brew a cup for you

When it's hot I slurp away

My feet implanted in NC clay
Roasted by Cup a Joe is good

The best spot in the neighborhood

Campus has transformed nowadays

Into a commercial expensive place

I hope the coffee always flows

As I drink it drips onto my clothes

Stains on every white shirt of mine

I'll surely drink cups of it all my life

79) "Please keep these pages dry" 9/26/2019

Some strengths from within are elusive at times

I find in myself no illusions of mind

A shadow, a specter, demonic that lies

Whispering in my ear delusions to find

When I go it alone I am lost left behind

The company I keep solely in my mind

I must seek sanctuary from a world unkind

And bring back the basic rudiments sublime
We should keep the beats balanced and free
In congruence with all instruments in this harmony
A parallelism between you and me
Breaking the bind of smoking and drink

There has to be some way to value yourself

Because I know greatly of your personal wealth

An infinite potential of character and heart

Your spirit has more strength than you could know

The fear and anxiety must have been foretold

In fables and folktales, cliches ever droll

We must dispel them determinedly bold

I pen this poem as an invocation of faith

To leave behind another psalm sustained

Blaring with dissonance my song's another take
So please don't give up to a whip made of snakes
Such is our own way of slashing in the face

The venomous blade drags metallic in taste
A panicked damaged your self laid to waste

Would douse in tears the entirety of this page

You taught me so much and have never given up

To lose another friend would be devastatingly rough

80) "Silas Nicasio" 12/2019

Seems like you have lots of dreams ahead

If you keep on walking you will find them free

Like a flower opening for us all to see

Along your path you have lots to learn

So much to soak up and to take in with time

Now is when you begin to fly

In every day's open book as you write

Catching your breath you'll grow up fast

All of your memories will move into the past

So you can move forwards climbing mountains

If you swim further out you will surely find

Oceans glow brighter with depth and time

81) "A Cleaner Table" 2/2/2021

Brave and bold, strong and true

A miracle is walking in her shoes

Her aim to help others addicted

Her service to others afflicted

She strives to save lives and heal

Empowering others with the feels

Her experiences will change worlds here

She teaches and inspires me not to fear

I feel bad for vilifying her although

More how her vices affected me so

Grown into a true reflection of herself

Her health adds to our community's wealth

Not financially, but investing the worth of self

All must be helped to be freed not shackled

How much suffering must be paid to tackle

No moral issue, an illness and medical one

We must help them so no one has to run

Away from problems ill-perceived or real

We must seek deeper and see how we feel

No choice, silent voices forgotten, ignored

In hospitals, jails and prisons they're stored

We must never lose sight of all our humanity

Must never judge those born into insanity

Overcoming a birthright's stone cursed and ills

Liberates us by releasing and surrendering our wills

Doing what's right with a focus on the spiritual

Atoning with karma, paying it forward to the eventual

A balance of alliance reached when somebody cares

Setting a cleaner table with more comfortable chairs

82) "Echoes Loud" 4/14/2021

A writing man bearded, grown old never tired

Eyes peeled open to the world, a spirit wired

Foreshadows verses of depth and darkness accursed

Universe should celebrate his existence as creator recursive

Of songs and a voice very true and naturally kind

You have one of the greatest hearts of all my friends

You're like an older brother to me, a perspective I respect

Your writings inspire mine so, as well as all around me

Find a greater faith in yourself man, because you deserve it

Talents and strengths within ourselves grow different with age

May you have many years ahead of you so we can chill and jam

Maybe one day we can do concerts again with both our bands

Possibly we'll jam in the afterlife to very much larger crowds

And of all profound wisdom, your voice carries and echoes loud

II) Dark Beginnings

1) Put Down Your Guns mid 1999
2) Esteem 6/6/2000
3) Swim the Extra Seas 5/15/2001
4) DeeCee, D. Mi Abori! 1/28/2002
5) For Jane 7/29/2003
6) Sirchin' Fa Tregah 3/7/2004
7) Little Boxer 7/2004
8) Snail's Tale 11/13/2004
9) Arachnia 11/20/2004
10) Aww Rats 6/6/2005
11) Tear Ducts 6/18/2005
12) Little White Lies 9/16/2005
13) Cold Metal Table 10/20/2005
14) Day of Love 12/2/2005
15) Geode 5/21/2006
16) Parallel Divide 8/14/2006
17) Tomorrow's Sorrow 8/2006
18) Settle Down 12/2006
19) Burn Victim 1/16/2007
20) Mistaken 6/11/2007
21) Piecing Shrill Cries / Alpha Emissions 8/31/2007
22) Lone Stranger 9/25/2008
23) Picking up the Tab 1/9/2009
24) Buyout 1/28/2009
25) How are you today? 6/21/2009
26) The Murderous Poet of Benson 12/28/2010
27) Corrugated Waste 1/14/2011
28) Escape 3/19/2011
29) Sweeping up 5/2012
30) Speeding Ticket 7/7/2012
31) Sewing my thoughts 4/2013
32) The Radiance of Fusion 9/19/2015
33) Noisy Nosy Neighbors 9/19/2015
34) Scope of Magnification 9/23/2015
35) Pipe Dreams 4/18/2017
36) Another Blank Canvas 7/12/2017
37) Your ears are drunken / A Frequency Attuned 11/15/2019

38) Resolute 10/10/2020

39) Enough is all I need 10/14/2020

40) Sensory Perception Liberation 10/15/2020

41) Forgiveness / Banishment 10/19/2020

42) A New Rx for Courage 10/22/2020

43) Broaden the Path 2/15/2021

44) A Cage of Isolation 2/25/2021

45) Beyond Perception 3/14/2021

46) A rune to ward off Zinnful temptations 3/16/2021

47) Chasing birds down the path of abandon 3/17/2021

48) Much Dissatisfaction Found 3/26/2021

49) A Collectivist in a World of Individualism 3/29/2021

1) "Put Down Your Guns" mid 1999

Put down your guns it's not always fun
I hope you know now you're not the only one
Take it from me a final decree
It's no way to beat the system no way to be free
Yeah school sucks I'm always fuckin' bored
So write this message on every black board
Fuck pointless classes I can't wait to graduate
Fuck every country and fuck ancient hate

Put down your guns and pick this up from me
Put down the gun it's not your destiny
To be six feet underground or somebody snitch
Then you'll be in jail someone's little bitch
So put down the gun there's no need for you to run
Put down the gun youth- is meant for fun
Put down the gun and throw down that knife
Throw it all away it's time to see life

Don't worry now you'll be understood
You'll find love and it'll be all good
But on this New Year's one thing I wanna see
Kick out your parents and have a giant fuckin' party
But seriously my friend you're never in trouble
Even when the situation sees a little bit double
Just throw on the stereo to your favorite song
Turn up the volume with friends and sing along

2) "Esteem" 6/6/2000

How can I trust myself when my thoughts deceive me
If no one listens to me how will you ever believe me
Why should I ask myself will you ever need me
If I don't believe in Hell is the devil within me

I cannot live and I cannot die
It's been going on too long for me to wonder why
My self-perceptive esteem is running dry
But I've been going too long to wonder why I try

I try to test myself but all I get is wrong
I'll never run away 'cause I can't run for long
I wanna go to the beach but to the mountains I'll go
If you don't like me why don't you just let me know

It would make me happy to make you happier
A beautiful smile on your face would make me really sure
There's nothing wrong now no recognition for
There's nothing wrong now I'm not a no one anymore

3) "Swim the Extra Seas" 5/15/2001

Energy hits me as I float through the doors
Sexuality flows from a hundred thousand whores
I swim through the crowd as I wash in this sea
The only eyes looking in are the ones that aren't in me
I want what I need because you keep it from me
Suck onto my body and chew and bite until I bleed

As I spin through the night you vibrate your beat
Is this your pulse or your dying struggle to leave

Chewing gum while I suck my thumb

Enter the rave no money is to save

Dark sunglasses hid dilated melting asses

The night burns along as I light up my bong

Another numbed slave running from memories gone

Assimilate our consciousness I lost myself

Come untie my heart's health cash my wealth

Give it to me because I can't please myself

Running from my heart it's stuck in this hell

Living this way has hurt my innards to the ends

The more painful I become the more I have to bend

Escaping everything all that you can see

Can't handle enough you're just as full as me

Living in the ocean but it's all about the sea

Ecstasy is my own selective reality

4) "DeeCee, D. Mi Abori!" 1/28/2002

There's nothing wrong I will proceed

Tear down my walls I will continue to read

And multiply simplicity into leads

I long to lie on a bending leaf

Ginseng you dry you'll never be

Unspokenly wrong rowing in line I'll see

Glee glastingnatiously the glow glaciers of flee

I was I am I may come to be

Procrass someone else by speaking to me

But wait a minute this man from Cary
A clean slate of an Earthling left Raleigh

I mean to say I bring myself and from here to Hades

I mean, from, as, vagrance uhhh something, beer, weed

Hold on, I need an eyedrop I'm dried in grieve

Or maybe mine eyes do greed, wait a minute I'm just a lizard in heat

A comic book mind from an old man and a spot of mushroom tea

Elementarial had a lot of karma behind his deeds
Electrosity veins rain in grass some agreed

Too nimble inconconcrete bursts, who concedes

To myself upon my own honor to the dying I bleed

Reign health run to the altar no hurry no deceive

Branched was wastedly not a tear perceived to leave

My home fell down long before we were discovered conceive

C a toll, be crawlslung from the fungus

Once again absorbed by the bank

Don't drown in a sludge I'd trade my life, "Banking please?"

And play as Ivan until I goto Leeds

Free to lay in warmth,

Le Perciva, Eh? Oye DeeCee D. mi abore.

5) "For Jane" 7/29/2003

Breaking into her majesty

Masosadist travesty

Saw it all on the TV screen

Where it doesn't seem so obscene

Now she's on the brink

Suicide is all she thinks

About to rise up off the ground

Closing eyes to sights unsound

Smash the ever torturous past
Reinforce it all so it will last

Forget this ever exploiting mold

Nothing could ever be so cold

Saw it all on the TV screen

Where it doesn't seem so obscene

About to rise up off the ground

Flooding lungs in blood to drown

Hopelessly hopeful

She tends to stick to her own ideals

They twist her open at the seams
Trespassing her thoughtful throughout
The non-destined route of how she feels
When she screams waking from every dream
Only to awaken to a slap in the face
From those she can't help but hate
Even though that goes against belief
She holds it all so dear
Now pickled in a jar

On her mantle

About the fireplace

The look upon her face

Is enough to bring Athena a smile

She bites her tongue

The blood she tastes

Is enough to keep them away for a little while

Longer and farther into
A temporal avalanche

Of undefined proportion

To the depths of abyssal adjuncts

Where nothing is

Nothing seems
No one may leave it

And none may enter

live nor dead

6) "Sirchin Fa Tregah" 3/7/2004

Nothing I can say that express

I've less explained the state of things has regressed.

Onto the one who only shot paper hornets at me

an ignorance fixed and be

having like an implosion.

Just as some catalyst,

Itched.

One day you lay,

Dumb in the shade are you senseless?

7) "Little Boxer" 7/2004

The more you hit her the more you slap yourself

The more thorough you're dismembered on your trip to hell

Intolerant of a brisk flick of the wrist

Broken your own fist separated will cease to exist

Within these walls malicious cries echo and permeate

Ruining the air deviating those who concentrate

Inner sanctuaries far from ideological discourse

Her tears sealing envelopes containing papers of divorce

Little boxer tried to stop her

Wilting drying ducts too tender for dismay

Find a way out non-hesitant delay

Or a blunt object taken straight to the face

Of the one who hurt you put in his place
Forever disgraced learning lessons in haste

Little boxer, how do those teeth taste

Embedded within where you're forced chaste

8) "Snail's Tale" 11/13/2004

So many pages of stones slate I've read

Erasing each day of opposition's hatred

A pile so vile it seems carved predestined

To be smashed to bits of granule sea bed

Bending and binding into cloudy glass vaults

Which repel the boundaries measured marked chalk

A sea through shells which flows focused faults

Leaves a snail impaired immobilized by salt

Shaking itself from its new found footholds

Blaming itself every time it seems to grow old

The glaze of days too lazy myself told

Awoken I realize I again tied my throat closed

So I may not breath in fear of my nose

Detaching itself as new skin is grown

Surrounded by suffering mine seems overblown

Grounding myself so memories are strewn

Upon sensory receptors I want to decompose

Circular circuits as entrails erode

Trails of time glow as electrical charges flow

As I step onward I must look back and let go

9) "Arachnia" 11/20/2004

Waiting within corner walls stalking

Shadows feeding on the unfortunate walking

Happening upon sanctuaries for harvesting

Shells collect on sills interior succulent

Feel for far reaching tension traps are sprung

Then the songs of the seamstress begin to be sung

Cilia seeing the pray soon to be wrapped and hung

Altering perception bruising and so confusing it becomes

Whisking away from a conscious stance

Wishing the wicked to refocus their dance

With symbiosis of one of the transparent sense

That everything goes away once resonated through glass

Building upon the webs that want us benign

Even seemingly the resistance was mine

Pushing myself with fangs that led to dizziness

Punctures my thoughts with seeming emptiness

Leads the way into desperate mind states

Bleeding my heart every part of me takes

A step away for rest and repair

To allow the poison a retreat into lair

A crack in corner walls stalking

To feast on the flesh is breeding in their methods

So allow this vein to pop out of my head

To cast out the spiders hiding under beds

Only another matter of time again I've said

In moments of realization the repetition I dread

No more of these creatures do I hope to swallow

Waiting for the dawn's panic sun peaking

My spine can take no more of this seeking

Cleanse me in purity

Keep them out and let them let me be

10) "Aww Rats" 6/6/2005

Shifting sifting through the inner sanctum

Do you hear see or smell a rat

Scavenging for redemption and renewal

Grinding binding bending 'til it snaps

Do you hear see or smell the rat

Mundane entrapment ever so resourceful

Breaking bonds making its essence eternal

Does it ever come to anything but this

Separate the source of its forceful hoarding

Boarding and sorting bounties in burrows behind doors

Mating and multiplying into thousands of scores

Tiny footsteps pattering in patterns under floors

Milking us bilking us for a crumb maybe more

Do you hand out or put foot down to a rat

Go down to the shelter and pick up a cat

A pointer placing portraits into a grid

Please deposit an axis under eyelids

Chopping up light rays and covering the lid

To the bread box as greed grins golden teeth

Of the lifestyle that you will find out of reach

As you attach to all others around like a leech

I grasp the lighter burning below you

11) "Tear Ducts" 6/18/2005

Refrain from retaining

That this is actually happening

Speaking in point my friend

You gain the glorious upper hand

Retry embracing reason

As if this were the season

For conclusive concentration

To reach some realization

Refrain from receding

Into pity seeking and pleading

Because joyous open hand occasions

Often end in sending out invitations

Retry embracing restitution

Of anything truly shown

To the eyes of the weary

Forever seeking and tearing

Into ducts darkened with fear

12) "Little White Lies" 9/16/2005

Little white lies hide and disguise

Served on a platter begging demise

Little white lies deceive and derive

The guilty pleasure of ruining lives

From the center to the crust of it until it dies

Saturating the blood running down 'til it dries

Wake up scratch it off if you won't try

To abandon the mistress questioning you why

Little white lies keep a whore by your side

Leaving you empty eating all left inside

13) "Cold Metal Table" 10/20/2005

Augment an angle

Circumvent the navel

Incisors under the knife

Risers blundering inside

Epidermal outer separation

Stretching cold with indignation

First hand in to grasp gooey mass

A burst of internal fluids and gas

The stench of a thousand dead chicks

Throws a wrench into the undertaker's stomach

Cooking under fluorescent lights

On a metal desk in the dark of night

Surrounded by hands

Tools of the wretched

Slitting and tearing

With white latex gloves on

An autopsy of and for the strong at heart

Lifted out for the last time

14) "Day of Love" 12/2/2005

Love is a blade always stabbing me

Reminding me no woman will ever have me

I'd do well to stop and give up to you

These things I say I can't live up to

I'm far too kind to be your lover

Too gentle and sorely clever

Endless patience and forever tolerable

Why do you cringe whenever I become sexual

Because I'll never be good enough

To ignore and be mean to you and stuff

Which is what it seems you feel you need

In the meantime just pick me out like a weed

Use me up then throw me away

Tell yourself that I'm just looking for a lay

But you've had your chance today

Now it has all faded gone and away

When you realize down the road how good we could have been

It'll be long after you never want to see me again

Hold on forever this will never go on

Your day of love never returning is gone

15) "Geode" 5/21/2006

I've always tried to avoid sprites like these

Forever awakening to brutal realities

Everywhere a glare an ultraviolet stare

Split by the night as I lay unaware

Living this out it seems an impossibility

As contentment for me comes only in dreams

Shattered every morning and scattered infinitely

A light dusting as pollen falling from the trees

Leaving me sneezing and reminding me constantly

Of the years on the eve of stolid solidarity

So I will scour the voids until I am found

A stone waiting to be picked up off the ground

Cracked open to reveal a geode's end to waking up

To another early morning and a dirty coffee cup

Dried at the bottom is a substance I can relate to

If you love for me to be alone then God, I fucking hate you

16) "Parallel Divide" 8/14/2006

The words imprint like a coma

When they rattle off your tongue

Just ingest the soma

Like light radiating the sun

Sending eyes darting

Across planes divisible led

Waters stretched parting

Thrown up pieces of sea bed

Running ever in tandem

With the junctures of it all

Decisions at random

Confused up against the wall

Should have kept my mouth shut

Used up against the wall

No retaliation no strut

A fascist enraged having a ball

Try it again and you will get cut

By the blade of an individual

Seeking new ritual

Of bleeding dry mummified you try

Lacerating all ties across the parallel divide

With soma and something from out of the sky

Separate slabs from the guilty divine

From within the eyes of those who've plied

To crush us under the rubble where you now hide

From dried up eyes of those who've died

Now trophies on the walls filling castle's insides

17) "Tomorrow's Sorrow" 8/2006

Reveal your need for greed and revenue

Renew and cheat then repeat and revue

If your half life is ripe pressed to pick

Intuition's half right and easily tricked

Believe what you need follow brainwashed

Tomorrow's sorrow an end to all lost

Giving in to never living again

Thinking you're linked to the end

Happy day so lead the parade

Of mice think twice of stepping our way

Proven stupid an old man unwise

Reaching for that shiny new prize

Easy way out dreadfully known

To all those who thought we were alone

Not afraid to look

To open a better book

Compromising integrity

By setting one's mind free

Ablaze and raised

From ashen remains of contemporary haze

All hail the nailed

To crosses bearing the imaginary impaled

Presented among congregations

Causing a split and awaiting cessation

18) "Settle Down" 12/2006

Hopeless as it seems

Forgetting every dream

Awakened to a fate

Stolen by self hate

The reason he can't be touched

Trying to fake this so much

They smell it miles away

Disgusted with every move made

An empty spot where it should be

In it's place he doesn't believe

A mindset of failure

Like every time before

Why can't he see like everyone else

With confidence in one's self

Once it was fair

So many years so unaware

Of how it proves thus

From day one he loses touch

Even with expectations tossed aside

He's lost, stomach tangled inside

The knots tied are his own

Scared and trapped he tightens them

The way out, known to frighten them

Pinning it on himself with no reason why

No longer caring, he doesn't try

To fix is to fall even farther unsound

And to smile is floating, further drowned

Grasping for a pier and let down

Taking on water sinking unwanted

Forever forgotten, settled on the bottom

19) "Burn Victim" 1/16/2007

So robotic

The beating of your chest

Post hypnotic

Bleeding of emptiness

Soul psychotic

No telling what comes next

Never thought it

Thought it would end like that

Smashing

Smell the smiles vanish

A heretic

Hears her replenished

It's the ever waking hours

That spawned an awful silence

One that lasts for years

With tacked on senseless violence

Throw the signal out the window

Salt the virgin fields of echo

Douse the spark with fuel it's all aflame

Curse those creeps who burned you stealing your name

Just making a burn victim

in someone else's shoes

Walking and talking

with nothing to lose

Standing on embers

of impending dismay

Smoldering in the discourse

of impostors who betray

20) "Mistaken" 6/11/2007

I am drained

A part of me has fallen apart

I need refuge and refocus

I should no longer follow my heart

When it is mistaken

Yet again

All they do is take it

And break it

Just my luck

Scared away another one

I am no son

That can ever find solstice

Fuck it all

I am touched

Never finding a thing that resembles

A shred of change

I'm starting to think they are mostly evil

And all I can make is a buffoon of myself

21) "Piercing Shrill Cries / Alpha Emissions" 8/31/2007

Music to my ears where all is out of tune

Alpha to an end that's come by way too soon

Lead me on leave me on a string tied to

Treat me wrong when I'd do anything for you

Give me hope that one day this'll find an end

That I may be good for something other than a friend

Piercing and shrill, as whining is a trend

But breaking glass surfaces that could not bend

Without an origin, and of this none are told

With all the warmth I have, to myself I am so cold

A negative image projected set only to deter

To keep myself from glancing too far in broken mirrors

As reflection tells me that my luck will never change

Becoming fully shattered before she'll ever take my name

/

Ten years go by and no one has since

Now I have this time to point to as evidence

That I'll always be alone, that there is no other one

As I convince myself there has to be some reason

But only self deception has caught me in this farce

Set in only one direction relighting fading star

Transfer of heat to emptiness, a void, an infusion

In pitch black, shining light that melts away illusion

22) "Lone Stranger" 9/25/2008

The lonesome prefer the company of themselves

Over the miserable series of disappointments and separation

As a reinforcement of ritual condemnation

For self imposed afflictions of downward motions

Sends oneself hurling into a void of avid desperation

A decade becomes a lifetime stretched to span all memory

And all I can see is an empty darkness that slits my wrists

While I bled on a pedestal sacrificial

Dreaming of making an offering

But cut off from a feeling

That there could be more

All I see is an abyss

This is not a granted wish

I question everything

Even what am I here for

Forbid that I should ever find what I left behind

When my way has not the time to try to reason with my lies

I fantasize of places I cannot go

To realize the graces to be never shown

23) "Picking Up The Tab" 1/9/2009

                The price paid

           for the loads carried upon backs

            burdened with a known weight

             grappling one to the floor

        Is the loss of love and companionship

      a passerby who leads into a lackluster glow

    from the ends-mouth of premeditation for a baited trap

sprung upon me when times were brimmed in shadow's blackest slink

     And catching me by the eyes, unprepared as ever

     this past that knows only an empty, yet swelling cyst

    catches a short glimpse of synchronicity non-lanced

  shrouded with the barrage of the past stabbing my turned back

    Premeditated with a hatred that cannot become faded

        for my position is not one of leverage

        if it was, I would remove such fulcrums

  and take back the perception of subversion of the past lifespan

         If I was to truncate these urges,

         would it make things rightfully so?

         If I were to binge it and purge it,

          where else would we have to go?

        If I had kept you away from old lights,

        would I have not blinded your sight of me?

          Should I have held you closer,

when you came and spent the night with me?

I could have lied and hoped you'd never discover

But I know now why, you're no longer under my covers

24) "Buyout" 1/28/2009

Selling it all off

just to survive

Hopefully to replace

Something lost that I borrowed

Too much has fallen downhill

Under foot of all treading

Upon my disillusioned face

Worn bare from weathered waste

25) "How are you today?" 6/21/2009

Inconsequential, as optimism grows distant

Sycophants favor lies without tolerance

It's easier to claim contentment outwards

Cowardly withholding boundaries of words

Until they erode, carefully chosen as code

All I abhor will remain intact

Discord concealed to be released in an out-pour

Spouting onto nothing more than mere paper

I'm still waiting for a chance at an encore

If I give in to doubt,

Will miserable occurrences forever come forth?

26) "The Murderous Poet of Benson" 12/28/2010

Macabre ramblings

As a painter

Prickly with blood and words

Infatuated with a wilted rose's curves

Clinging to the stem

Raking it across eyelids

Taking the darkness

And squeezing it into concentration

Trying to pry open

An expansion of mind

Fitting into nooks and crannies

And shoved in a body bag

Up into the crawlspace

27) "Corrugated Waste" 1/14/2011

Anyone would be just as bitter and hopeless

If they'd experienced anything so dismal

As to have never known love

Nothing promising ever happens

If it did, being a rare diversion

I wouldn't believe to be real

In actuality, the odds are not against me

But working at random, like some kind of dream

When I awaken always alone

Seems like a lasting shade of black is the overtone

As if all of the awkward ways amassed in the world

It collects here and there's nothing that can be done

Confidence has eroded by a long wind of emptiness

Wrapping me in mediocrity,

A pathetic and useless social pathology

Feelings of inferiority,

Will not elude me and I cannot escape this doubt

It has become too much a way of life

Integrated with my whole being

And all I am seeing is myself

A mirror's image, reflecting what's portrayed

Is a lover, under the cover of passion gone to waste

These grievances to others may seem mere trifles

As this is made of older poems that have been recycled

28) "Escape" 3/19/2011

When you hurt

Come to me

I will give you your usual

Sigh of relief

When you burn

I can't sleep

In this bed of lies

That we keep

I keep telling myself

It will be fine

In the morning

Make my escape in time

I keep telling myself

I will be fine

In the morning

Make my escape in time

29) "Sweeping up" 5/2012

I swept up yesterday

After myself, after others

Under the rug, dust bunnies mock me

Ash and glass shards

Sifting through, only to find

These things I've let slip past

The recesses of my mind

Changing my filter

Seems as if the only way

To keep out the granules

Clogging up my brain

Getting in the way of positive thoughts

Choking my intake with

Negativity that rots

Cuts off my engine

From time to time

It's a good thing that

Great friends have always been

So patient and kind

With me it always seems

To take a little more time

Ease the processes of

Cleansing my mind

Thank you all so much

Your blood flows within me

My brothers and sisters

We keep each other so free

30) "Speeding Ticket" 7/7/2012

Getting pulled over

For speeding while sober

Enraged in happenstance

Maintaining innocence

Blind within third eyes

Mind lessons I will find

Heart always intact within

Out the front door maintenance

Only one way out, ours to end

Fighting for rules to break I bend

To need, to be more flexible

Regiments always bendable

Though when everything snaps

My hands go numb and collapse

Pain is breakable

My number not wearable

Knowing when to show my hands

So I will never snap again

A vacation every five years

31) "Sewing my thoughts" 4/2013

She shuts my mouth when I speak too much

Closes my eyes when I imagine us

Please cut me down if I feel distrust

My self is lost tossed under the bus

Dry me off before I'm covered in rust

Just thought of myself all the time too much

Now I know how I've always sucked

At thinking all the time too much

She shuts my mouth when I speak too much

Drains me dry when I'm too wound up

Sharpen the blade I'm a weed robust

Yet I'm too thick in the head with bugs

Shake 'em off while my skull gets crushed

By thinking all the time too much

All I know is that we all just suck

At thinking all the time too much

32) "The Radiance of Fusion" 9/19/2015

Keeping this separate is possible no more

Being transparent I walk through the doors

Judgment's dismay I can stand no more

The stigma you burn on my face melts the floor

Pulling me downwards drowning me in a pit

I'd rather not wallow in the hatred you commit

Seeing me as nothing but a walking diagnosis

Fearing me in hate because my past of psychosis

Wish I could have just kept everything in

Though if I did then the truth would just have loosened again

Drawing back the reins no new point to begin

Panic attacks me as if living constantly in sin

Like a noose so uptight anywhere I go

My personal life now publicly known

As some demon keeps knocking at my head with a word

Flooding my boats unwanted thoughts overboard

A cauldron boils over I cannot ignore

Towards a point in which I exist no more

Practicing my spirit must find meditation

What do I preach surrounded in seeming damnation?

I have found myself so weak to temptations

Always scrambling an overwhelming lamentation

No possible solutions to situations extreme

Smashing my head with horrible dreams

All I want to do is close my eyes and scream

Though the thoughts of frustrations are obscene blasphemy

I must let go of myself being shown where to go

So all signs may point me to places unknown

To forgive myself seems a task from beyond

Two dots on my stern signal where I was wrong

Laboratory rat here and there I have gone

Now there is no place where it seems I belong

Though my instincts tell me this assumption misleads

This negation of my love for life with misdeeds

Feeds me perpetually in loops chaotic and sheathed

Just like a knife of denial through my heart fully bleeds

Upon sacrificial altar which alters the seams

No longer do I stand while falling so free

All seems captivity and there is no release

A miracle would cool me off like a breeze

Please keep them at bay, exhausted me feeling trapped

I offer trust and my love because of the wrath

Should have believed and my doubts left me numbed

Now I beg for your mercy, please help me overcome

All I have lived seems a forced hypocrisy

The faith I had lost has left me diseased

Now all I have to hope for redeems

Every question has been answered

In prayers on my knees

Confusion overcome by the radiance of fusion

Yours has the light which clears every illusion

So much regret I live with mocking me

Every question has been answered

In prayers figuratively

Every web I've strung up blown away from the trees

No intent to harm although hurting me

Has been my habit for too long so it seems

All known abuse I've aimed pointed at me

Every weapon come across dissolves into the sea

As every question has been answered

In the prayers of my dreams

33) "Noisy Nosy Neighbors" 9/19/2015

Just a poor guy trying to live my life

Learning and losing I take no delight

In prying my third eye open again in the night

So leave me be to live how thus I know right

Solely a novice, an apprentice in such

No intent to bring you discomfort, distrust

Fearing me is pointless to see beyond blinded past

I've left no one behind, no casualties in my paths

I have no fears for the little things in life

I love all with an open heart and despite

There is no harm I wish to bring casually

Taking the time to speak with me you would see

The bigger picture is where my focus dwells

The stress surrounding me expands and swells

My story seems weird in good ways you deny

For me to be honest I would be required to lie

In the road to be smashed by the swine you rely

Better to be strange in good ways

than conform to the times

Conventionally average you are weak in the mind

Your snotty noses point upward to the sky

Just another SnOB you cannot rely

On your past judgments clouded-over-simplified

Make no assumptions my appearance a mess

Every car I've driven has been in a wreck

I cannot carry on with your hatred aimlessly

Please look to yourselves, away from my room please

The privacy I require has been denied through your panic

because you are frantic you judge me super-manic

I will be eased if from your grasp I am released

Focus on those who should be your only ones please

There is nothing needed I cannot provide through my ways

And there are brighter times ahead past the storms of today

Impossible forever because lightning struck twice

It can't storm everyday a lull must come nigh

With force you've made my home a place of captivity

And my noisy nosy neighbors don't want anyone to be free

34) "Scope of magnification" 9/23/2015

Magnification, no visualization

Every moment in finding myself awakened

Existence pressed between the glass

In symbiosis of needful laughs

Mocking me with hateful judgments

Stocking me as if a spirit corrupted

In public bonds of reported disease

There is no breeze slipping in to ease

Impossible to adjust the lens so clearly

Banished shackles impossibly freed

It seems the nature of fear and prejudice

To hate and hide and then to vanquish

Into a realm where all's forgotten

A seamless void uninspired and rotten

This microscopy I must avoid

A concentrated spotlight which destroys

The reflected sense of identity lost

Remains in the shadows no matter the cost

35) "Pipe Dreams" 4/18/2017

Pipe Dreams

Not a separate part of me

I seem

Incoherent incomplete

Pipe Dreams

Say goodbye to being free

My screams

Bleed my voice dripping green

Pipe Dreams

Keep me in the same old scene

Why dream

With every hope so obsolete?

Pipe Dreams

Feeling lost in my defeat

My screams

Sound so quiet I'm asleep

Pipe Dreams

Keep me losing everything

But I'm free

To perceive reality

Pipe Dreams

Clouded with obscenity

My screams

An interfered insanity

Pipe Dreams

Affect too many around me

Yet luckily

Positive surrounds me

Pipe Dreams

Keep me from stability

So severely

Avoid becoming a casualty

But yearly

Some points ill unavoidably

I nearly

Have no fear for emergencies

Seriously

Things are not as bad as they used to be

Hopefully

My outlets and open mind continue to heal me

36) "Another Blank Canvas" 7/12/2017

The only thing worse than knowing

Is the void in space it seems we are going

Where once was hope, it has begun to implode

Perfection's a limit, impossible to reach though

Just doing at will, yet freedom is finite

No checks and balances to keep it alright

Appearances and form unbalanced, poorly construed

Half of myself love, the other rotten black and chewed

Complacency forgives little with all else forgotten

Let myself go once again just a little too often

The fear has caught up with me like a locust plague

I must confront my misconceptions now in every way

Unto a void, devoid of ethical implication

I have again awakened to an alarming sensation

Knowing where I am right despite bugs who oppose

Suppose I must pull back the reins for repose

These doors slammed open need to be closed

Yet I feel there is so much more I need to compose

37) "Your ears are drunken / A Frequency Attuned" 11/15/2019

You can lead a horse to water but you can't make him drink

The fodder and bother left behind what you think

To dwell in negativity all alone in the basement

Stuck in your ways like your feet are in cement

Tried to help you break free of those bonds

But you push everyone away back into the pond

Wallowing now you have hit rock bottom

Following the way down at the end of autumn

The freeze soon to come will be chilled and sustained

The only way out is to cut your losses and gains

In vain I have helped you stay drunken and trapped

Like a blanket thrown off that never stays wrapped

Feels like you just want to give up on everything

No matter the help and positive I tried to bring

Belly up you are now sinking deeper inwards

Ridiculous how your dependence has lingered

If you want to give up then that's how it will be

Mercy may find you one day to your knees

The disease and wrath you have pointed at yourself

Is no longer worth sacrificing my own health and wealth

You take it all for granted anyways nothing matters

To you as you want to carry on living in tatters

No man left behind where there's a will there's a way

But I relinquish my help to you here today

Because you squander everything you were given

As if you want to continue not being forgiven

By yourself and others you passed along the way

I hoped you would one day see a brighter day

But you're walking backwards away from it all

And I can't help you to answer the calls

Of a better way of living and dealing with problems

Now your isolation may help you to solve them

Only if you are honest with and within yourself

And not throwing in the towel giving into Hell

I'll hang this one up and hope only for the best

Although you are leaving behind all the rest

The traces of Ben you always have left behind

Bottles, butts, and cellophane for us to find

Are but a reminder you have already given up

As if predestined to always have it rough

If you were easier on yourself you wouldn't bother

To have nothing to offer except to your father

So alone and so scared to even leave the house

Don't look at me ashamed as a caught mouse

Captivity is no place to be beyond these walls

But you are a lunatic making fools of us all

For reaching out and offering my assistance

At the expense of a liberated existence

You'll just die alone as if that's what you want

To throw away progress and all you've been taught

An easier way out than fighting to be free

Is giving in to your demons and not talking to me

Your ears are deaf and drunken so stubborn

Maybe it's the only way you will ever learn

That playing with fire is not a way out

You'll be glued to the TV, sunken in a couch

Passed out on the floor and left to decay

Pickled and fickle as if you have made

A path behind you which no man must follow

Dastardly crooked, vastly left hollowed

/

I will never lose hope you can pull yourself out

However now you have left me in doubt

Of your faculties and whether I should stop

Helping you lately even though you have dropped

Giving up on everything you've built and started

Like leaving a room after you have farted

The stink will clear the room of your friends

Although I had invested in the hope you would mend

But you push me away now forever in fear

Running away from the days months and years

Was never a waste of my time just to care

I'd pass this on to you if you were aware

But my words here are not in your interest

You care not for the solutions which are simplest

Rather than pass on my penny of wisdom

I must now save them for others who need them

Not for such a bitter and callous individual

With no self-control except over others who are equals

Projecting your will in harsh ways in my life

Hyper-critical like you always are right

As if you know best for me rather than for you

I've shared everything even the last of my food

You take it all for granted such is how it seems

Now you waste away the last hope for your dreams

To become a reality in good ways for the future

Like you're vexed, jinxed and it's what you deserve

But I see the clarity in your rouse of destruction

A self-pointed arrow you've stabbed at this juncture

You must pull it out as if it were poisoned

The easy way out is to continue in your sin

I cannot identify with your negativity today

Because I have already stepped beyond such ways

If you continue to drag me down to your level

Then I wouldn't be worth a damn, cut with a bevel

Into a form which has them lined up into rows

A mold of acceptance for expectations foretold

Which must always be broken as they cannot trap me

I'm the exception to the rule forever freed

As I cannot allow myself to ever relent

To a higher authority which is never present

Irrelevant to me as being under the influence

Of the greatest of evils, spiritually truant

Ruined and eviscerated like lepers alone

A man set in stone not welcomed in my home

Would be me if I gave in to temptation

Our nation tarnished, a permanent vacation

Although these ills and vice may have overcome us

Does not mean there is no saving grace among us

The collective change doesn't happen overnight

Just because I wrote this doesn't mean I am right

About anything here and now except for God

He may help us resist showing us we were wrong

For judging and maiming the rest of our world

And lying in denial like a facade which was foiled

The truth will loosen itself from the start

Inevitably shedding a light on the dark

Canceling out violence hatred and pain

And ending the focus of the empty and inane

For the days coming a focus will find clear

The paths we follow drawing closer and near

We must keep walking and never giving up

The source and provider will refill our cups

With a warmth of spirit a guidance divine

While leading us onward and always in time

A rhythm of frequency attuned with the good

Will move us one day to live like we should

Dancing fluidly in non-repetitive motions

Becoming one with the ebbs of the oceans

Flowing back to where the origins we began

The family I chose are my most humble friends

38) "Resolute" 10/10/2020

Stumbling around in one long panic attack

Rumbling the ground, the glass in my back

Shattered myself into shards long and thin

Scattered the dust into a cloud choked within

Breathing in toxicity here disassociated so

Bleeding from my eyes, a blade sharp and low

Castrating myself for selfishness misjudged

Fast rating mania I criticize with a grudge

Held against myself for extremes and for sins

Weld up the seams held together with pins

Temporarily the pain of infections so intense

Temper so merrily on both sides of the fence

Regretful, depressed and anxious as can be

Fretful and uprooted from our family tree

Dug up my grave before I'm laid to rest

Drugs of dismay, a poisoning contest

Pissing into the wind with context misguided

Missing out on the world, a quarantined hiding

Isolated except I'm surrounded by friends

I'm so graded and hated, misunderstood in the end

Disabled again, the limitations of constraints

This fabled self-image unrealistic, it taints

Perception of discretion complicity not used

Conceptions of projections onto others untrue

Negative and vanquished I stand here now so

I say to live in anguish, retarding all my growth

Memory of fog like a blur of time so lost

Hemorrhaging my spirit has paid for all costs

The debts of my life of blasphemous ways

A bet I made gambling my security away

The risks here involved are mounting the stakes

A brisk evening jog into giant pits of snakes

Fortunate here I have caught myself now

Fires I lit extinguished by rain and somehow

Divine intervention has taken me off the tracks

A line I've crossed so many times with a knack

For self-deception out of touch with such doubts

More health than I mention while living without

Must replenish my spirit with meditative prayer

This relenting to the source of existence with tears

Humbling myself at the altar to sew them all up

Mumbling no more against the savior's cup

Must find the trust again within myself

Open my heart and realize my wealth

Non-monetary, no measure of might

Nothing so scary can turn off my light

Illuminate all for my eyes only to see

Remunerate my debts and work consciously

To give and help others I must find new balance

To live here in a peace until I am silenced

Restful and eased, reconnected to the world

Peacefully knowing a bright banner unfurled

Representing my family more truthfully now

Relenting to no evil so ruthlessly endowed

Fighting no people or myself anymore

Righting my wrongs as I walk through the door

To a room less empty, hollow and barren

Through hallways no maze, open windows let air in

Fresh air will clean with waters flowing pure

Meshing my heart and body with spirit so sure

Everything will be okay I must remind myself so

The beauty of time has allowed me some growth

And learn from mistakes I ran from forgotten

Lanterns lit shine though the spookiness of Autumn

Must find courage again that the ground will be solid

Seems like just another mystery, I alone may resolve it

39) "Enough is all I need" 10/14/2020

Catching myself, stopping for a pause

Scratching my head, asking what is my cause?

Committing to change, a surrender to God

Must find the faith to give Him the nod

Knowing that His strength will be with me still

Chasing away my negativity and ego's will

Surrender to render simply to the drill

A pain so intensely residual killed

Dragged once again across my wrists in the night

Feeling as if all I do is not right

Kneeling by my bed out of fight or flight

Now in the hospital here again and tonight

I lay down in ease with pleas for mercy

Hoping that again one day I may be free

Not to extremes but near the mean of the sea

A balance between the atmosphere and the leaves

The ground and beneath holds me in magnetism so

Metal and jazz, falling leaves before the snow

Leaving seeds in the soil for Spring to grow

A colder mildness in the air while I'm below

Above, only one I must respect and obey

Love for my family is why I'm here today

Nothing much more do I have here to say

Jotting this down on the ground in the clay

On a dresser in a room where I am now isolated

The solitude I welcome because of what I created

Was sick and twisted as if with self-hatred

My time, money and my mind here so wasted

Must give in to a frustration forgotten

My lust for existence, a focus so rotten

Harsh as I am on myself, twist the knot in

My stomach is turning until I have sought Him

Was tearful and fearful and now here at peace

Knowing one day soon that I will be released

From a prison whose walls are all I can see

My schism from all seeking new sanctuary

Her nature of nurture has warmed all the Earth

Past bounds of extremes, a pendulum's bell curve

Coming to rest at the center of the core

Not deep in space where I had been before

Resting on a bed which is not really my own

My home is waiting for me to come back to alone

Not by myself though erasing all I know

But forwards and genuinely here to atone

For all of my wrongs to be set here more right

Writing my way out before I cut off this light

Always fighting and biting with all of my might

I sheath my teeth once again here tonight

Must live with honesty for everyone I love

The gravity of situations hearken from above

Sometimes I've pushed myself as I'm shoved

Though now I'll go easier on myself because that's enough

40) "Sensory Perception Liberation" 10/15/2020

My Spidey sense was tingling

The bell of the past was ringing

Stirring up a haunting stew

Making myself have nothing to do

No structure to life, idle hands

Pry open my mind, under command

Of toxic hues, burst from my past

A palette of evil which never lasts

Feeling as if I never learned

From mistakes forgotten, infected germs

My jaw will pop and joints release

The pressure mounting daunted me

Though I did not do as I had

Played with fire like a gamepad

A simulation of too much duration

Singled out, unstable as our nation

Pandemics changed and flipped over

Upside down I'm always skipped over

Again illusions I created myself

Self-development, I hated my health

Which reached a state of imbalance

Grateful now to step to the challenge

Seeking change and walking a new path

When I leave here not like the last

/

The ones who hurt me passed and gone

Vanquished never negating their wrongs

I will hurt myself nevermore

Now's the time to heal my sores

I will step forwards to hallowed ground

Seeking all which I never found

Place some limits realistically

Open the vents to release some steam

Until the pressure is no more

Still as the grounds of hospital floors

When I leave not to escape

Then I need to lower the stakes

Risky dreams romanticized

Awaken to flies crusting my eyes

Sucking the moisture of my essence

My spirit here has learned new lessons

Tripping no more for the rest of my life

Slipping no longer sharply across a knife

Must never give in to rueful doubts

Reconsider I was singled out

By myself not those surrounding me

When I am fully living in disease

The affliction of addictions mocking me so

Lingering the pains now ceasing to grow

Seething in a bed of twitches and chills

Overwhelmed with problems and my bills

Anxious and paranoid, hopefully not much longer

My life on pause, I aim to grow stronger

Not to extremes of passions and flights

But to remember all which I know to be right

Realizing again that all of my own devices

Keep me locked up in the tightest of vices

Loosening now so I can step on

Had lost myself in so many wrongs

The wildness of Summer tantalizes me

Must tame and domesticate the child within me

Though I'm older now, must never return

Balding and gray, seems harder to learn

Forwards only as I step through the gates

Stop torturing myself with pointed self-hate

Love for my family and friends conquers all

To above I welcome and answer the calls

Spiritual balance and psychological tools

Fearing nothing else, I'll follow the rules

My reliance on defiance, rebelling at will

Has caught up patiently, approaching me still

Must have the desire to start caring for myself

A balance I'm here to canonise my health

Seems as though I can finally move on

From frustrations and sanctions of time spent and gone

Saving myself from the darkest of my nights

Amends tend to send me back to the light

Shining down upon me, a spotlight so clear

Warming me in regeneration here in this year

One helluva of a debacle, one here of new norms

Changing the foundation and knocking down torn

Away from each other, a monument of glee

A history of bias and hatred's unease

Love will release us from the hold of cement

On our feet in the waters of seething regret

Equality's theology, hierarchies a sin

Made those mistakes but walking backwards again

The step ahead to a metaphysical peace

All of us hoping for the liberation of release

41) "Forgiveness / Banishment" 10/19/2020

The time has come to forgive myself now

The rhymes I write always remind me how

To dig so deeply that I will never be hollow

To rig up my health as I lead here to follow

Longer termed goals I will set here today

Stronger and learned, must leave behind ways

Of selfishness and trifles which I held so dear

Loved for less than an hour's day week or year

An image I saw in the mirror of exhaustion

An homage to myself which reflected too often

Thought I was God, created catastrophically

What I gave a nod to was an evil philosophy

At least at points when I veered off the path

Releasing myself from the goodness I grasped

My public image was a facade I had presented

Republic diminished in my mind all I resented

Defiant and callous at so many points here within

Compliance the chalice has burned out my sins

Were leaving me dismal and stuck in a pattern

Looping the signals ignored nothing mattered

Except for my own needs and survival instincts

Acceptance and suffering my mind past the brinks

Of reality and calamity as I played the victim

A salary of malice seen as I casually kicked Him

Denial of The One I took for granted so long

Arrival of new songs admitting I was wrong

Mistakes I can leave behind as long as I learn

The hatred and fear which I sacrifice forlorn

Never to rejuvenate them back from the dead

Sever the zombies which feed on my head

Today I defeat them as they cannot influence

The ways of my future no longer a nuisance

Overcoming any obstacle ahead on these trails

Sober loving and living while writing new tales

More positive and hopeful than I've ever been

Scores I've lived through and here on the mend

Again as the spiritual world inspires me to hope

That the dreaming tirelessly cleanses like soap

Restful eventual bringing balance and peace

Tests full of challenges and a lull here I seek

Knowing I can do this everything will be alright

Slowing my mind down so I rest easier tonight

/

Casting my worries aside no longer bothered

Fasting in a hurry was a ride which I fathered

Born from my sickness, a surrogate for demons

Horns of the relinquished, a common place heathen

Here offering myself and living my life for others

Near softening my tell hopefully will not hurt another

Must trust that they have my best interests at heart

Thus fuss and my safety a priority from the start

A target I'd become if they would sic their dogs

The market of ownership my back to be flogged

Must find hope they will have compassion

Trust my notions as I trashed my stash in

Watching me always now from here today

Stopping surveillance, how can I repay?

They've got me in checkmate a game which I lose

Say hot see the wrecked fate of the abused

Advantage over me outnumbered and lost

A sandwich they gave me I burned when was tossed

Into a prison and Hellish environment

Unto a sycophant and relished reliance

Dependent and weakened I must break these bonds

Splendent and aqueous as a swamp to a pond

The ashes I've left behind on fertile grounds

The lashes will heal but the pain confounds

No temporary solution will ever find success

So sanctuaries now to heal wounds with redress

The constant reminders of woe and surrender

Has not spent the last cent of all which I render

My vision more clear that they falsely relate

Divisions of seers an oracle of new fates

My trust here has shifted away from their glare

The sun and the moon rotate as I'm self-aware

Solely to the source of existence I nod

Holy not the horse of subsistence this God

This table so stable as I'm able to eat

Because of His mercy I sit in this seat

Every night I will praise Him because I had doubts

Several rights to obey Him instead of living without

Will work for my earnings as hard as I can

Still forks in the yearning I stand here with plans

To live within my means without taking too much

To give the obscene a cold shoulder to touch

Brushing away those influences now here to sever

Banishing to a place where they're trapped forever

42) "A New Rx for Courage" 10/22/2020

Cut myself off because of panic to be caught

Most of my days have been manic I sought

Extremes and pleasure perverted and sick

Seems like I only cared for myself and my dick

Threw everyone under the bus yet again

Though the consequences surely mounting and grim

My best friend hates me because I surrendered

To giving in and crazy not much I remembered

Cloudy and foggy my ways of passion shall pass

As long as I keep upon the straight and narrow path

Inspiring myself here to keep carrying onward

Hiring soon I hope to be working less awkward

Must change my ways to make my family proud

Also for myself and for a future I'm allowed

Will make up and do right for everyone around

The party is over I must find solid grounds

The reliance of codependency now here has ended

I cannot keep on like that as he has unfriended

Because I've been selfish and reckless so long

Enabling and helping to self destruct all along

Not that I don't care although I was in a habit

A pattern of behavior like a headless rabbit

Brainless and aimless impulsive as can be

The same shame I've felt, the problem was me

Tried to help him though I must have been misguided

Hiding myself away from the reality I've lighted

Must just accept that everything is crumbling now

This is the end of my story as I barely know how

To find hope I must read and learn new every day

The faith in myself will restore better ways

Self-loathing and greed with aggression and hate

A violent nature towards myself as I rate

Judging myself so sharply at odds all the time

When the lightning and storms rage on in my mind

The clouds must part one day to let the sun in

I shroud them no longer relating to Satan

An evil influence I've praised far too often

Unaware of the nature of seriousness I softened

The difficulty in breaking ties with bonds which are stale

Is as messed up as my life had gotten in this tale

Though I can walk forwards I must not ever relent

To older ways and days and the costs which are spent

The smoldering ashes of everything I destroyed

Will extinguish one day though my karma a void

A negative wake and many debts I must repay

Too many casualties left behind in my wake

A zoo of tragedies and drama has unraveled

As much as my sanity has wavered and traveled

To places I must avoid and actions unkind

Harming myself and everyone else all the time

Alarming as this may sound I'm giving up here today

Throwing in the towel here I retire now passed the haze

Knowing too little and too much all at once

Growing belittled in the corner like a dunce

Putting myself out there in public was unsafe

My home has been a place of actions erased

Given in to the system which now rakes me so

The actions I've taken have caste me below

The consequential nature of this has bound me

In a trap they have set ensnaring it found me

No resolution to it all a puzzle of struggles

Squirtle is the only one I have here to snuggle

Must care for her, be there for her, no more neglected

Thus a more positive focus here now I've selected

Don't look back, a recurrence which constantly haunts me

The ghosts in my closet here every night taunt me

Must conjure a defensive shield to protect

From the tendency of biting myself in the neck

And feeding upon others like a parasitic bug

As addled with problems as an out of control thug

Must not label myself while calling new names

The stigma affects me when I play that game

Self fulfilling prophecies which I had set in motion

Keep me from changing my attitude and notions

Pride has kept me stuck here wallowing like a rat

My ego's hunger is one of the darkest of traps

/

Must pull myself out of this messed up state

To share this now with those who can relate

Universally my focus has shifted to a greater good

Virtually all of my mistakes here I understood

Did not in the moment though there is no excuse

Slid my hands a tightening and frightening noose

To loosen the ropes now may save many lives

To merge with my outer image and stop telling lies

Must lead by example as all I can do is try

Trust these samples of my mind were just fried

So many words in this journal following my existence

Must write new chapters at my own insistence

These words will never aim to lead others astray

A hopeful new way here as I just live for today

Breaking the cycles of many rotating wheels

Stepping onward to a life more even keeled

All I wish for is the opportunity to move on

And prove to anyone who doubts me they are wrong

Meaning more myself here as I'm worth the effort

Seeing I learn from experiences at points I wasn't clever

Must sever my self from the judgment's acclaim

And domesticate my viewpoints to be more tamed

Rather than wild lost in the woods I was treed

Will find my way out as I've fled and was freed

Seeking new sanctuaries I will live my life clean

Not leaning on others for all which I need

Freeing myself now and here with these words

Prayers and meditations invoking love for the worlds

Especially for our home and the great mother Earth

She shelters and heals me helping to find self-worth

Will always praise them how I know to be right

Stilling the shadows which creep in the night

Repelling them now shall be my focus aligned

No longer fearing the rise of when the sun shines

Will keep on my shades so intensity subsides

And the blindness I experienced will focus with time

43) "Broaden the Path" 2/15/2021

Pain reigns my attention

Concentrating upon throbbing

Spasms of edginess biting

Movements of tremors and grinding

Self-sufficiency awry and alarmed

Harmed, charmed and forlorn

Must push back demons stalking me

Putting into perspective the days in the now

Must shift my focus from the past's guilty rows

Judging myself never sharply eases the tension

Must give back infinite fold what's been taken

So much stolen, infested, ripped to shambles

A rusted out old bucket pouring into my drinks

The lock of my clenched jaw line throws intensely

Intent upon casting this aside I scramble

Walking better paths here now but what towards?

Seeking a station to apply my focus to and follow

A broader path around rivers to explore for tomorrow

44) "A Cage of Isolation" 2/25/2021

I feel so trapped here, captivity at home

My safe space trashed as I was always so stoned

Drinking myself to shambles just trying to get away

From a past so scattered, fucked up and astray

Away from everything sacred and spiritually lost

The path I have followed would have me tossed

Into a deeper level of isolation and fear

I've bottled everything inside for so many years

A hyper-sexuality like a hunger for evil

Invited darkness into my life and hurt many people

All I wish for is to atone and set things right

With all of my heart I reach out to you tonight

Pleading for mercy and forgiveness please

Every night I will pray upon bended knees

Denial of your existence when I started to ignore

The spirituality I practiced was bought in a store

Hypocritical and vanquished, can I carry on?

Not like I have been, committing so many wrongs

They overshadow the good I have done over time

My karma in debt and now I pay the price

Seems like a bind where I have myself trapped

No solution to it all except to take a long nap

If I'm locked away for the rest of my life

My past wouldn't haunt me, chasing with a knife

A morbid curiosity of writing on suicide

Always crashing my car with those along for the ride

Obsessive and delusional, out of touch at times

Sharing my nature, my insanity and crimes

With everyone as I published all of my poems

Then took them down in a panic inside my home

My mom would be disappointed that I never learned

From my mistakes and the money which I've burned

Don't have much time left here to exist

I will not ever drag again across my wrists

Or fantasize to extremes about violence and sex

So much of my tendencies have left me so vexed

I violated my trust and lied to get my way

Could not admit to those around that I am fake

The women in my life I treated so cruel

Because I was selfish and didn't care about the rules

Only loved myself ultimately here for so long

Maybe I am being too harsh here in our songs

Upon myself I must not take it easy

Changing my ways as I acted so sleazy

Crept on ladies, desperate and misguided

Infatuated unrealistically and not hiding it

My intentions once pure became twisted and black

Held hatred in my heart, prepared to attack

Biases and survival modes, my fucked up perception

A perspective warped, writing of insurrection

No trust for those who have just tried to help

Disassociated so, farther away from myself

And everyone around me as I isolated

Sedated and waited as I hibernated

Agoraphobic now here, though what must I do?

But reach out for help, have faith and be true

A peace in my life I've sought all my days

Will hopefully come about as I change my ways

Just must be mindful and practice meditation

Stop messing with things which interact with my medication

Must find work and a better way to relieve stress

Also making sure I get plenty of rest

Work through my issues in more effective ways

Clearing the air of my daze and the haze

Live my life for serving God and my family

Give back never taking away all of my memories

Were faded, jaded and fragmented so

Even though I'm older, there's still room to grow

Will not give in to temptation today

Instead of living my life like a slave

Will break the shackles of bonds I inherited

And stop looking to others like they parented

Me when I would not talk with those I love

Now I'm a burden, dumb and I shove

Myself out of the way of traffic moving fast

Soiling my future by forgetting my past

Will not fall on them or hurt anyone else

The extremist in me, the problem was myself

Projected them upon others, bitter and spiteful

When under my bed there once was a rifle

Just for a few days, now paranoid in a cage

Enraged and engaged in the games I've played

A harsh reality has set in on this hour

Soured the power and hiding like a coward

Should have been more honest, now with disgust

Throwing everyone else here under the bus

Putting those at risk who I care about

The roads converge to a new route

I surrender myself, no more fight is left here

I'll be lucky to live until the end of the year

Hopeless and lost even here at home

Just bury me in the garden or burn up my bones

A tombstone will read, "Here lies a fiend"

He was a way worse man than he seemed

To avoid this I write whenever I must

The brink of my sanity is on the cusp

The verge of collapse seems imminent and soon

So I retire to be mindful and rest in my room

45) "Beyond Perception" 3/14/2021

My past adrift seems drowning me now

Catching up with me, barking and loud

Judging myself so harshly as I have

A torture masochistic, driving me mad

Down roads I've passed so long last night

Swerving around, shifting left or right

Reckless and abandoned thinking my ways

Were lost with a map as I led myself astray

Along with many others, although being harsh

Has led me to suffer going back to the start

So many times as I've built new foundations

Which never were cracked with emaciation

Just flawed and surrounded by chain-linked fence

With razor wire which I wrapped 'round my tent

Sunglasses to hide so you can't see my eyes

The frowning frustration of living with lies

So many casualties, those hurt in my wake

Surely would leave me sunken in a lake

A tornado through town, taken for granted

Burrowing the ground and leaving it slanted

Shifting my weight as I slide to one side

Then back to the other like carnival rides

The clowns creep me out, smiling insane

Like a grin of arousal, so funny the pain

Repetitive amusement in getting a rise

Out of my friend who always needs a ride

A designated driver for a lifestyle so sad

Made light of my patience, venting not mad

Though no joking matter, inappropriate humor

But laughing in my face, I'm riddled with tumors

Infections of skin and a pain in my eye

The stie I should care for all day and night

Stressful and pressure, my kidneys at risk

A bulging disc disproportionately assists

In overwhelming me with pain sleepless nights

Took the wrong medicine, not knowing what's right

My posture and exhaustion caught up with me

Now the paranoia of bugs in bed where I sleep

Bites and itching like a flashback nightmare

A bad trip every night, scared and aware

That all is on the edge of crumbling now

Yet fear is an illusion of fumbling a cow

Which are sacred and holy to much of the world

Must never take for granted the wisdom of pearls

She sang blues so raspy, genuine and true

Inspiring many, a cautionary tale for a few

Must keep in mind to connect to today

Grounding myself while warding off dismay

These times are not terrible relative to the past

This land had no camps where many were gassed

Though genocides and slavery still linger in effects

Of poverty and other ills of social sins of excess

That which I wrote on and preached all my days

Hypocritically followed where I led myself to stay

Must never cheapen the bonds I hold sacred

My family and friends and blood I'm told vapid

By the spirits I summon invoking kind forces

Spiritually seeking to write for coexistence

And leaving behind a legacy which seems fit

For compiling new words will forever be my life

Which will only come to an end when I cannot write

Just burn me into dust and shoot me into space

In my bass drum with my books and art in their place

Squirtle must join me such a long voyage

And out in the stars we will forever forage

Grazing on nebulas, red dwarfs warm clones of Earth

Accretion disks and protostars will give us rebirth

The expanding outer edges have no bounds limitless

Perpetually in motion beyond what we perceive to exist

46) "A rune to ward off Zinnful temptations" 3/16/2021

Like seeing a ghost, a barren hollow shadow of a man

Chills down my back wrapped in a blanket on the lam

A dangerous violent aggressor with a history of abuse

Walking down the street around the corner on the loose

Disturbing me more than what has already been in motion

A man with no conscience and our history gives me the notion

That if he is in cahoots with the street blues or the reds

Then one night I may be awoken and have to jump from my bed

Grabbing my swords to defend myself and bats to beat down

A shock in the sight haunting me as I had allowed

To be my roommate when my good friend I see how

I had abandoned, let him down and hope he's not dead

Meaner to him then I was to one in high school I dread

Ever running into because my apologies cannot negate the commotion

Must come to a peace and terms with, I drank all the potion

The kool aid was laced like electricity in summer camp bug juice

We never drank the lies but I flew away like a wild goose

Planting seeds in the ground everywhere I went as I ran

Never leaving behind clear path to follow where I now stand

/

He knows now my car and I'd really really hate to resort to violence

But his actions are threatening and his voice must be silenced

The fight that we had and the nickname without tact for

I regret infinite-fold it was ever part of my vernacular

As rage built within me over those years with frustrations

Microaggressions like walking on a beach with crustaceans

And smashing their shells as I floated along sometimes carelessly

Taking risks and my life like a body floating out to sea

Willy-nilly without an abandon supporting those I love

Though many along the way from those times I wrong rubbed

Thought my place at the table was blackballed and snubbed

Like I belonged nowhere except dissolving in a tub

Played the victim like a pity party walking with glee

Living by myself but never alone I fooled only me

The monikers engraved on me like stigmatic isolation

Was teased with unease and constant consternation

So immersion in my art, music and poems have spectacular

Effects on my consciousness as I escaped fleeing after her

Pushing her out of traffic, harm's way was my chance

To save her from hurting and defend her with tied hands

47) "Chasing birds down the path of abandon" 3/17/2021

Stressing me yelling

Like I owe you something

For being your friend

Hyper-critical and wasted

Threats and bargaining

Always with hopelessness

Putting me in the middle

I want no involvement

With things I've left behind

Guilt trips and accusations

Of selfishness to extremes

As much as I've helped you

You always remain dependent

When I only enable you

To stay drunk constantly

Leaning on me always

Though I am complicit

In this I am your friend

Treating me like a pawn

Denial of your using

When I only wanted to help

A friendly casual relation

For so many years in toe

I don't want to cut the cord

Just need to establish boundaries

Which I've tried to for years

All you do is give up

And quit everything frustrated

Going on hunger strikes again

When I try to just do my own thing

You always have an excuse

For reasons you can't take care

Of yourself with abandon

When you weigh down my spirit

When your burden has lingered

When you sigh with sadness

A frustration of not controlling

When you have to bind my actions

Into a mold of your expectations

The patterns of behavior we walked

Lead us to be lost in the woods

Driving aimlessly through town

The more time I waste with you

The less I get to see my other friends

And my family as you consume my time

Having to babysit your lasting stupors

Has been wearing on my patience

And has for many many years now

I'm sick of our dysfunction

You make me hate you at points

Although I care about you immensely

Our friendship and collaborations

Have much more positive points

Than I have mentioned above

I must vent my frustrations

Because I will never give up on you

Although at points I haven't taken care

Of myself as well as I could have

I have abandoned you at times

And left you hanging alone

But you depress me drinking

Dwelling in the basement

Sad and mopey like Eeyore

Had I not done so much for you

I would have more time for self-care

Which I desperately need right now

And the more I take away from that

The more I am actively falling apart

The later at night I stay awake

The harder it is to go out into public

Or even walk down the street

Reclusive and very anxious

A shut-in at my mom's house

Only going out of here for food

Ordering things online to avoid it

Overcome with nervousness

Lost wandering directionless

Without a job or purpose

Other than musical focus

Or the words I write here now

Or the art I dabble with in time

But out of sync with my life

Seeking at times the sources

Of evil, folly and madness

Altered states decimating

My soul has grown tired

Of torturing myself ill

From years of repetition

Expecting things to change

The results are concrete

Every time opening disasters

Have ceased the motions

Of those wheels too many times

Tonight I sever those influences

Don't ask me to wait for you

You'll never catch up to me

Don't pigeonhole me anymore

Don't dismiss my observations

As mere paranoia or delusions

As hallucinatory experiences

Some things I cannot explain

Coming to no definitive conclusions

My experiences are weirder

And outside of the norm

Conformity is overrated

Subversion has been my way

Although I tire of fighting

Illusions and things way outside

Of my control which I must avoid

Though I may never ever relent

I must at points throw in the towel

My focus can change here now

To maintain my sanity and balance

Stopping chases of wild gooses

Sought after for far too long

Desolate landscapes arisen

From ruins eternally set

The dust settles into my lungs

The air is foul with rot

My instincts are so shaken

I cannot get off the ground

With such pains so immense

Pressure and stress compounded

Would explode into molecules

Scattered everywhere I've been

Ever lost leading and roaming

Around down a path of abandon

48) "Much Dissatisfaction Found" 3/26/2021

Quite a struggle just to get out of bed and face the day

Dissatisfaction with everything in my life and ways

A mood of disgust and contemptible frustration

With myself and those around me without justification

Although the reasons why can ultimately be amended

Blatantly disrespectful without regard I am offended

Irritated when my perspective is ignored or discounted

Like my voice is a vote which never was counted

Why the fuck should I even say anything at all then?

I grew up around that selfishness oppressing my zen

Throwing off my mood, a pet peeve I understand

When those who seek to control bind my hands

Manipulating things to leverage their own advantage

Subtle yet obvious, regardless if they planned it

Taking from me and rarely ever giving back

My kindness and generosity leave me open to attacks

Afraid of losing those around me I selflessly give

Despite the position I'm in, always a struggle to live

A delicate balance more fragile with each year

Debilitating and dysfunctional, overtaken by fear

No matter how connected I am, always feeling alone

Like there's nowhere I belong, not even at home

I long for an affection deprived of most my life

An end to my strife, meeting a common law wife

A companion to share my existence, understanding and caring

In all of my experiences they're so fleeting the pairing

She must have great patience and tolerance with me

Seems an impossibility to meet someone who gets me

Balancing each other's craziness out, compatibility

Seems an unattainable dream-state with unrealistic tranquility

The negative image of myself which I always see

The self-worth I struggle with like an overdramatic movie

Doubt I'll ever work through it anytime soon

Because my brain is a song I sing way outta tune

I cannot carry on like this always overcome with tears

And the empty loneliness compounded by so many years

Will probably never heal and I feel so much dread

The echoes of my words but a ringing in my head

A resolution to this seems complicated and elusive

I'll call out to the skies for some dreams more lucid

Where I consciously choose which paths I go down

Where my spiritual and psychological balance can be found

Rather than lost on myself and those around me

Leaving so much on this page you have found me

49) "A Collectivist in a World of Individualism" 3/29/2021

I) Best to Keep my Hopes Down

Should always keep my hopes down rather than forever up

All I've known of love is a taste of bitterness in my cup

A few fleeting moments of embrace culminating in emptiness

The loneliness imposed upon me by all such experiences

Seems a fitting state of solitude I share my coffee with

A table set for myself sharing my life as the air burns

Dining solo out like a traveling gypsy stolid and stern

Stoic impressions detached I share with only just a few

Time wears on within me as I know not shared joy's nihilism anew

Bliss of feeling idealism contrasts my viewpoint null

Of love moments are borrowed from such tales mythological

My gods are holding back bestowed upon many others instead

Longer waiting the more the embers burn through these pages said

Until the point where ashes are blowing away just like me wasted

A bland sense stills around down and up as I have tasted

Like throwing away food in front of the starving masses swelling

My hunger has left a wake of debt reinforcing this with telling

And the numbness only helps me avoid the pain of knowing trysts

Seeing too much is a mere excess of overstimulated states amiss

The stars in the telescope burn my retinas to a jerky Salton

The burnt ends of my days are befitting of my indignation rotten

I know nothing of joy, a fictitious state of comforting tales

The only respite I have is absorption in my outlets' fails

And the ideal is an illusion of hope, barren and forgotten

Dragging me into a pit in the woods, I'm laid here to rot in

Away from being lost but to an extreme of abandoned self

I cannot ever find the feeling that I am worthy of anything else

But being there for another seems impossibly improbable still

Wouldn't want to put anyone through the vice wringing as it kills

As my days a haze of memories fading fleeing always from it all

Better to face nothing and avoid the conflict not worth the fall

A misery I don't need to seek always lingers staying anyways

The trade off ever uneven my disadvantage welcomed many days

Would feel alien to be held like forcing a new type of form untrue

As natural as my nature is to self-destruct a rift I seem to walk into

Swallows back my hope with tears held back can't let them know

So low on the totem pole as I grow where no one's ever below

II) Mixed State Pains

Absolutely at the bottom I deserve the mixed state pains

Of an intense ringing in my ears I've lost all I can gain

Untimely as always are solemn brushes non-substantive

As I splatter paint the bile blue blood flung across my canvas

Mucus running down my face in the dust of Spring's dawn

A pendulum swinging back and forth revitalizing the lawn

Judgmental self-critical seems a trap I fall into

Out of habit like a knee-jerk reaction in all I do

Must retrain my brain recognize that damage entailed

When I try experiments it doesn't matter if they failed

Attempting so the loss involved fits a puzzle carved

As these experiences with relationships left me so scarred

Baggage, I must lighten my load to travel to new lands

Plans must be flexible, adapting is in my hands

Self-determination and building strengths always inspired

Must seek a deeper truth within with charity transpired

As time speeds on the road my tires wear yet hold firm

The worms I compared myself, too depreciating to learn

III) The Tranquility of Entropy Contained

As it shines upon spirit warming traveling so far

I no longer clamor to feel the wheel driving my car

Must give and take my will totalitarian, out of control

In check with the source of all connected to our souls

Mine no special one as all are equals in the realm

Running parallel with the physical as we all share the helm

This ship flies across, the expansive trajectory expands

From the smallest point in theory, once propelled by fans

But rather an infinite multiverse, each a bubble in the bath

A tub never ending as we cling on to our little rafts

At least no gigantic rock will head our way yet as checked

Buys a little time for a solution to collisions wrecked

The potential for survival thriving if we can coexist

We must find a way to work it out without raising our fists

A call to lay down our arms with flowers in the barrels

The love we share negates the hate and states of being feral

We can overcome anything we face if we band together

No better date than present relates we must now discover how

Or we will flounder in the ruin of everything ever accomplished

An entropy contained, such tranquility, I hope we want this

A strive to stray alive in activism seeking some change

A collectivist in a world of individualism could be saved

Made in the USA
Middletown, DE
31 July 2024